THE GOSPEL WORTHY
OF ALL ACCEPTATION

The Gospel Worthy of All Acceptation

The Duty of Sinners to Believe in Jesus Christ

Andrew Fuller

CountedFaithful

THE GOSPEL WORTHY OF ALL ACCEPTATION

First published in 1785

This abridged edition published in 1837
This edition © Counted Faithful, 2020

COUNTED FAITHFUL
2 Drakewood Road
London SW16 5DT, UK

Website: http://www.countedfaithful.org

ISBN
Book: 978-1-78872-248-3
ePub: 978-1-78872-249-0
Kindle: 978-1-78872-250-6

Contents

Contents

Preface

WHEN the following pages were written the author had no intention of publishing them. He had formerly entertained different sentiments. For some few years, however, he had begun to doubt whether all his principles on these subjects were scriptural. These doubts arose chiefly from thinking on some passages of Scripture; particularly the latter part of *Psalm 2*, where kings who *set themselves against the Lord, and against his anointed,* are positively commanded to *kiss the Son:* also the preaching of John the Baptist, Christ and his apostles; who, he found, did not hesitate to address unconverted sinners, and that in the most pointed manner; saying, *Repent, for the kingdom of heaven is at hand – Repent, and be converted, that your sins may be blotted out.* And it appeared to him, there must be a most unwarrantable *force* put upon these passages, to make them mean any other repentance and faith, than what are connected with salvation.

Reading the lives and labours of such men as Elliot, Brainerd, and several others, who preached Christ with so much success to the American Indians, had an effect upon him. Their work, like that of the apostles, seemed to be plain before them. They appeared to him, in their addresses to those poor benighted heathens, to have none of the difficulties with which he felt himself encumbered. These things led him to the throne of grace, to implore instruction and resolution. He saw that he needed both; the one to *know* the mind of Christ, and the other to *avow* it.

He was for some time, however, deterred from disclosing his doubts. During nearly four years they occupied his mind, and not without increasing. Being once in company with a minister whom he greatly respected, it was thrown out as a matter of enquiry, Whether he had generally entertained just notions concerning unbelief. It was common to speak of unbelief as a calling in question the truth of our own personal religion: whereas, he remarked, "It was the calling in question the truth of what God had said." This remark appeared to carry in it its own evidence.

From this time his thoughts upon the subject began to enlarge. He preached upon it more than once. From hence, he was led to think on its opposite, faith, and to consider it as *a persuasion of the truth of what God hath said;* and of course, to suspect his former views concerning its not being the duty of unconverted sinners.

He was aware that the generality of Christians with whom he was acquainted, viewed the belief of the gospel as something presupposed in faith, rather than as being of the essence of it; and considered the contrary as the opinion of Mr Sandeman, which they were agreed in rejecting, as favourable to a dead or inoperative kind of faith. He thought, however, that what they meant by a belief of the gospel, was nothing more than a general assent to the doctrines of revelation, unaccompanied with love to them, or a dependence on the Lord Jesus Christ for salvation. He had no doubt but that such a notion of the subject ought to be rejected.

It appeared to him, that we had taken unconverted sinners too much upon their word, when they told us that they believed the gospel. He did not doubt but that they might believe many things concerning Jesus Christ, and his salvation: but being blind to the *glory of God,* as it is displayed *in the face of Jesus Christ,* their belief of the gospel must be very superficial, extending only to a few facts, without any sense of their real intrinsic excellency; which, strictly speaking, is not faith. Those who see no form nor comeliness in the Messiah, nor beauty, that they should desire him, are described as *not believing the report* concerning him. (*Isaiah 53:1, 2*).

He had also read and considered, as well as he was able, President Edwards' *Inquiry into the Freedom of the Will,* with some other performances on the difference between *natural* and *moral* inability. He found much satisfaction in this distinction, as it appeared to him to carry with it its own evidence, to be clearly and fully contained in the Scriptures, and calculated to disburden the Calvinistic system of a number of calumnies, with which its enemies have loaded it; as well as to afford clear and honourable conceptions of the divine government. If it were not the duty of unconverted sinners to believe in Christ, and that because of their inability, he supposed this inability must be natural, or something which did not arise from an evil disposition: but the more he examined the Scriptures, the more he was convinced that all the inability ascribed to man, with respect to believing, arises from the aversion of his heart. They *will not* come to Christ, that they may have life – *will not* hearken to the voice of the charmer, charm he never so wisely – *will not* seek after God – and *desire not* the knowledge of his ways.

He wishes to avoid the spirit, into which we are apt to be betrayed when engaged in controversy, – that of magnifying the importance of the subject beyond its proper bounds: yet he seriously thinks the subject treated of in the following pages is of no small importance. To him it appears to be the same controversy, for substance, as that which in all ages has subsisted between God and an apostate world. God hath ever maintained these two principles: *All that is evil is of the creature, and to him belongs the blame of it;* and *all that is good is of himself, and to him belongs the praise of it.* To acquiesce in *both* these positions, is too much for the carnal heart. The advocates for free will would seem to yield the former, acknowledging themselves blameworthy for the evil: but they cannot admit the latter. Whatever honour they may allow to the general grace of God, they are for ascribing the preponderance in favour of virtue and eternal life, to their own good improvement of it. Others, who profess to be advocates for free grace, appear to be willing that God should have all the honour of their salvation, in case they should be saved; but they discover the strongest aversion to take to themselves the blame of their destruction, in case they should be lost. To yield both these points to God, is to fall under in the grand controversy with him, and to acquiesce in his revealed will, which acquiescence includes *repentance towards God, and faith towards our Lord Jesus Christ.* – Indeed it were not very difficult to prove, that each in rejecting one of these truths, does not in reality embrace the other. The Arminian, though he professes to take the blame of the evil upon himself, yet feels no guilt for being a sinner, any further than he imagines he could by the help of divine grace given to him and all mankind, have avoided it. If he admit the native depravity of his heart, it is his misfortune, not his fault: his fault lies not in being *in* a state of alienation, and aversion to God; but in not making the best use of the grace of God to get out of it. And the Antinomian, though he ascribes salvation to free grace, yet feels no obligation for the pardon of his impenitence, his unbelief, or his constant aversion to God, during his supposed unregeneracy. Thus, as in many other cases, opposite extremes are known to meet. Where no grace is given, they are united in supposing that no duty can be required; which if true, *grace is no more grace.*

The following particulars are premised for the sake of a clear understanding of the subject:

First, There is no dispute about the doctrine of election, or any of the discriminating doctrines of grace. – They are allowed on both sides; and it is granted that none ever did, or will believe in Christ, but those who are chosen of God from eternity. The question does not turn upon what are the causes of salvation, but rather upon what are the causes of damnation. "No man," as Mr Charnock happily expresses it, "is an unbeliever, but because he will be so; and every man is not an unbeliever, because the grace of God conquers some, changeth their wills, and bends them to Christ."[1]

Secondly, Neither is there any dispute concerning who ought to be encouraged to consider themselves as entitled to the blessings of the gospel. Though sinners be freely invited to the participation of spiritual blessings; yet they have no interest in them, according to God's revealed will, while they continue in unbelief: nor is it any part of the design of these pages to persuade them to believe that they have. On the contrary, the writer is fully convinced that whatever be the secret purpose of God concerning them, they are at present under the curse.

Thirdly, The question is not, whether men are bound to do anything more than the law requires; but, whether the law, as the invariable standard of right and wrong, does not require every man cordially to embrace whatever God reveals: in other words, whether love to God with all the heart, soul, mind, and strength, does not include a cordial reception of whatever plan he shall, at any period of time, disclose?

1. *Discourses*, Volume 2, page 473.

Fourthly, The question is not, whether men are required to believe any more than is reported in the gospel, or anything that is not true; but, whether that which is reported ought not to be believed with all the heart, and whether this be not saving faith?

Fifthly, It is no part of the controversy, whether unconverted sinners be able to turn to God, and to embrace the gospel; but what kind of inability they lie under with respect to these exercises? Whether it consists in the want of natural powers and advantages, or merely in the want of a heart to make a right use of them? If the former, obligation, it is granted, would be set aside; but if the latter, it remains in full force. They that are in the flesh *cannot* please God: but it does not follow that they are not obliged to do so; and this their obligation requires to be clearly insisted on, that they may be convinced of their sin, and so induced to embrace the gospel remedy.

Sixthly, The question is not, whether faith be required of sinners as a virtue, which, if complied with, shall be the ground of their acceptance with God; or that on account of which they may be justified in his sight: but whether it be not required as the appointed *means* of salvation. The righteousness of Jesus believed in, is the only ground of justification; but faith in him is necessary to our being interested in it. We remember the fatal example of the Jews, which the apostle Paul holds up to our view, *The Gentiles,* saith he, *which followed not after righteousness, have attained to righteousness, even the righteousness which is of faith. But Israel, which followed after the law of righteousness, hath not attained to the law of righteousness.* WHEREFORE? BECAUSE THEY SOUGHT IT NOT BY FAITH, *but as it were by the works of the law. For they stumbled at that stumbling-stone.* (*Romans 9:30-32*). Though we had not been elsewhere told, that in doing this they were *disobedient,* (*1 Peter 2:8*), yet our judgements must be perversely fixed, if we did not conclude it to be their sin, and that by which they fell, and perished. And we dare not but charge our hearers, whether they will hear, or whether they will forbear, to beware of stumbling upon the same stone, and of falling after the same example of unbelief.

Finally, The question is not, whether unconverted sinners be the subjects of exhortation, but whether they ought to be exhorted to perform spiritual duties? It is beyond all dispute, that the Scriptures do exhort them to many things. If, therefore, there be any professors of Christianity who question the propriety of this, and who would have nothing said to them, except that, "if they be elected they will be called," they are not to be reasoned with, but rebuked, as setting themselves in direct opposition to the Word of God. The greater part of those who may differ from the author on these subjects, it is presumed, will admit the propriety of sinners being exhorted to duty; only this duty must, as they suppose, be confined to merely natural exercises, or such as may be complied with by a carnal heart, destitute of the love of God. It is one design of the following pages to show that God requires the heart, the whole heart, and nothing but the heart; that all the precepts of the Bible are only the different modes in which we are required to express our love to him; that, instead of its being true that sinners are obliged to perform duties which have no spirituality in them, there are no such duties to be performed; and that, so far from their being exhorted to everything excepting what is spiritually good, they are exhorted to nothing else. The Scriptures undoubtedly require them to read, to hear, to repent, and to pray, that their sins may be forgiven them. It is not, however, in the exercise of a carnal, but of a spiritual state of mind, that these duties are performed.

1

The Importance of the Subject

GOD, having blessed mankind with the glorious Gospel of his Son, hath spoken much in his Word, as it might be supposed he would, of the treatment which it should receive from those to whom it was addressed. A cordial reception of it is called, in Scripture, receiving Christ, allowing him, believing in him, and so on; and the contrary, refusing, disallowing, and rejecting him; and those who thus reject him are, in so doing, said to judge themselves unworthy of everlasting life. (*John 1:12; 3:16; Psalm 118:22; Matthew 21:42; 1 Peter 2:7; Acts 13:46*). These are things on which the New Testament largely insists: great stress is there laid on the reception of the truth. The same lips which commissioned the apostles to go and *preach the Gospel to every creature*, added, *He that* BELIEVETH AND IS BAPTISED SHALL BE SAVED; BUT HE THAT BELIEVETH NOT SHALL BE DAMNED. *To as many as* RECEIVED HIM, to them gave he power to become the sons of God; but to them *who received him not*, but refused him, and rejected his way of salvation, he became a stumbling-stone, and a rock of offence, that they might stumble, and fall, and perish. Thus the Gospel, according to the different reception it meets with, becomes a *savour of life unto life, or of death unto death.* (*Mark 16:16; 1 Peter 2:8; 2 Corinthians 2:16*). The controversies which have arisen concerning faith in Jesus Christ, are not so much an object of surprise, as the conduct of those who, professing to be Christians, affect to decry the subject as a matter of little or no importance. There is not any principle or exercise of the human mind of which the New Testament speaks so frequently, and on which so great a stress is laid. And, with regard to the inquiry, whether faith be required of all men who hear, or have opportunity to hear the Word, it must be of great interest. If it be not, to inculcate it would be unwarrantable and cruel to our fellow-sinners, as it subjects them to an additional charge of guilt: but, if it be, to explain it away is to undermine the Divine prerogative, and, as far as it goes, to subvert the very intent of the promulgation of the Gospel, which is, that men *should believe that Jesus is the Christ, the Son of God; and, believing, have life through his name, (John 20:31)*. This is, doubtless, a very serious thing, and ought to be seriously considered. Though some good men may be implicated in this matter, it becomes them to remember, that *whosoever breaketh one of the least of Christ's commandments, and teacheth men so, shall be called the last in the kingdom of heaven*. If believing be a commandment, it cannot be one of the least: the important relations which it sustains, as well as the dignity of its object, must prevent this: the knowledge of sin, repentance for it, and gratitude for pardoning mercy, all depend upon our admitting it. And, if it be a great commandment, the breach of it must be a great sin; and whosoever teaches men otherwise, is a partaker of their guilt; and, if they perish, will be found to have been accessary to their eternal ruin. Let it be considered, whether the apostle to the Hebrews did not proceed upon such principles, when he exclaimed, "*How shall we escape, if we neglect so* GREAT *salvation?*" And the Lord Jesus himself, when he declared, "HE THAT BELIEVETH NOT SHALL BE DAMNED!"

In order to determine whether faith in Christ be the duty of all men who have opportunity to hear the Gospel, it will be necessary to determine what it is, or wherein it consists. Some have maintained, that it consists in a persuasion of our interest in Christ, and in all the benefits and blessings of his mediation. Others, who would not be thought to go so far, for the sake of many Christians whom they cannot but observe, upon this principle, to be, generally speaking, unbelievers, yet maintain what fully implies it. Though they will allow, for the comfort of such Christians, that assurance is not of the essence of faith, understanding by assurance, an assured persuasion of our salvation; but, that a *reliance on Christ* is sufficient; yet, in almost all other things, they speak as if they did not believe what, at those times, they say. It is common for such persons to call those fears which occupy the minds of Christians, lest they should miss of salvation at last, by the name of unbelief; and to reprove them for being guilty of this God-dishonouring sin, exhorting them to be strong in faith, like Abraham, giving glory to God; when all that is meant is, that they should, without doubting, believe the goodness of their state. If this be saving faith, it must inevitably follow, that it is *not* the duty of unconverted sinners; for they are not interested in Christ, and it cannot possibly be their duty to believe a lie. But, if it can be proved that the proper object of saving faith is, not our being interested in Christ, but the glorious Gospel of the ever-blessed God, (which is true, whether we believe it or not,) a contrary inference must be drawn; for it is admitted on all hands, that it is the duty of every man to believe what God reveals.

I have no objection to allowing that true faith has in it the nature of appropriation; if, by this term, be meant an application of the truths believed to our own particular cases. "When the Scriptures teach," says a pungent writer, "*we* are to receive instruction, for the enlightening of *our own* minds; when they admonish, *we* are to take warning; when they reprove, *we* are to be checked; when they comfort, *we* are to be cheered and encouraged; and when they recommend any grace, *we* are to desire and embrace it; when they command any duty, *we* are to hold ourselves enjoined to do it; when they promise, *we* are to hope; when they threaten, *we* are to be terrified, as if the judgment were denounced against *us;* and when they forbid any sin, *we* are to think they forbid it unto *us*. By which application we shall make all the rich treasures contained in the Scriptures wholly our own, and in such a powerful and peculiar manner enjoy the fruit and benefit of them, as if they had been wholly written *for us*, and none other else beside us." [1]

By saving faith, we undoubtedly embrace Christ *for ourselves*, in the same sense as Jacob embraced Jehovah as *his* God, (*Genesis 28:21*); that is, to a rejecting of every idol that stands in competition with him. Christ is all-sufficient, and suited to save *us*, as well as others; and it is for the forgiveness of *our* sins that we put our trust in him. But this is very different from a persuasion of our being in a state of salvation.

---

1. Downame's *Guide to Godliness*, page 647.

My objections to this notion of faith are as follows:

Nothing can be an object of faith, except what God has revealed in his Word: but the interest that any individual has in Christ, and the blessings of the Gospel, more than another, is not revealed. God has nowhere declared, concerning any one of us, as individuals, that we shall be saved: all that he has revealed on this subject respects us as *characters*. He has abundantly promised, that all who believe in him, love him, and obey him, shall be saved; and a persuasion, that, if we sustain these characters, we shall be saved, is, doubtless, an exercise of faith: but whether we do them or not, is an object not of faith, but of consciousness. "*Hereby we do know that we know him, if we keep his commandments.*" "*Whoso keepeth his word, in him verily is the love of God perfected: hereby know we that we are in him.*" "*My little children, let us not love in word, neither in tongue; but in deed and in truth. And hereby we know that we are of the truth, and shall assure our hearts before him.*" (*1 John 2:3, 5; 3:18, 19*). If anyone imagines that God has revealed to him his interest in his love; and this in a special, immediate, and extraordinary manner, and not by exciting in him the holy exercises of grace, and thereby begetting a consciousness of his being a subject of grace, let him beware, lest he deceive his soul. The Jews were not wanting in what some would call the faith of assurance: *We have one Father*, said they, *even God:* but Jesus answered, *If God were your Father, ye would love me.*

The Scriptures always represent faith as terminating on something outside of us; namely, on Christ, and the truths concerning him: but, if it consists in a persuasion of our being in a state of salvation, it must terminate, principally, on something within us; namely, the work of grace in our hearts; for to believe myself interested in Christ, is the same thing as to believe myself a subject of special grace. And hence, as was said, it is common for many who entertain this notion of faith, to consider its opposite, unbelief, as a *doubting whether we have been really converted.* But, as it is the *truth* and *excellence* of the things to be interested in, and not his *interest in* them, that the sinner is apt to disbelieve; so it is these, and not that, on which the faith of the believer primarily terminates. Perhaps what relates to personal interest may, in general, more properly be called *hope* than faith, and its opposite, *fear*, than unbelief.

To believe ourselves in a state of salvation, (however desirable, when grounded on evidence,) is far inferior, in its object, to saving faith. The grand object on which faith fixes, is the glory of Christ, and not the happy condition we are in, as interested in him. The latter, doubtless, affords great consolation; and the more we discover of his excellence, the more ardently shall we desire an interest in him, and be the more disconsolate while it continues a matter of doubt. But if we be concerned only for our own security, our faith is vain, and we are yet in our sins. As that repentance which fixes merely on the consequences of sin, as subjecting us to misery, is selfish and spurious, so that faith which fixes merely on the consequences of Christ's mediation, as raising us to happiness, is equally selfish and spurious. It is the peculiar property of true faith, to endear Christ: *Unto you that believe*, HE *is precious*. And, where this is the case, if there be no impediments, arising from constitutional dejection or other accidental causes, we shall not be in doubt about an interest in him. Consolation will accompany the faith of the Gospel: *Being justified by faith, we have peace with God, through our Lord Jesus Christ.*

All those exercises of faith which our Lord so highly commends in the New Testament – as that of the centurion, the woman of Canaan, and others – are represented as terminating on his *all-sufficiency* to heal them, and not as consisting in a persuasion that they were interested in the divine favour, and, therefore, should succeed. *Speak the word only*, says the one, *and my servant shall be healed. For I am a man under authority, having soldiers under me: and I say to this man, Go, and he goeth; and to another, Come, and he cometh; and to my servant, Do this, and he doeth it.* (*Matthew 8:8, 9*). Such was the persuasion which the other entertained of his all-sufficiency to help her, that she judged it enough if she might but partake of the crumbs of his table – the scatterings, as it were, of mercy. Similar to this is the following language: – *If I may but touch the hem of his garment, I shall be made whole. – Believe ye that I am* ABLE *to do this? They said unto him, Yea, Lord. – Lord, if thou wilt, thou* CANST *make me clean, – If thou* CANST *do any thing, have compassion on us, and help us, Jesus said, If thou* CANST *believe, all things are possible to him that believeth.* (*Matthew 9:28; 8:2; Luke 5:16; Mark 9.22, 23*). I allow that the case of these people, and that of a sinner applying for forgiveness, are not exactly the same. Christ had nowhere promised to heal all who came for healing; but he has graciously bound himself not to cast out any who come to him for mercy. On this account, there is a greater ground for faith in the willingness of Christ to save, than there was in his willingness to heal; and there was less unbelief in the saying of the leper, IF THOU WILT, *thou canst make me clean*, than there would be in similar language from one who, convinced of his own utter insufficiency, applied to him for salvation. But a persuasion of Christ being both able and willing to save all them that come unto God by him, and, consequently, to save us, if we so apply, is very different from a persuasion that we are the children of God, and interested in the blessings of the Gospel.

That the belief of the truth which God hath revealed in the Scriptures concerning Christ is saving faith, is evident from the following passages: – *Go, preach the Gospel to every creature. He that believeth and is baptised shall be saved.* Believing, here, manifestly refers to *the Gospel* to be preached, and the rejection of which would subject the unbeliever to certain damnation. – *These things are written, that ye might believe that Jesus is the Christ, the Son of God; and that believing ye might have life through his name.* Believing unto life is here described as a persuasion of Jesus being the Christ, the Son of God: and that on the ground of what was written in the Scriptures. *Those by the wayside are they that hear; then cometh the devil, and taketh away the word out of their hearts, lest they should believe and be saved.* This language plainly denotes that a real belief of the Word is connected with salvation. Peter confessed, *Thou art Christ, the Son of the living God. Jesus answered, Blessed art thou, Simon Barjona: for flesh and blood hath not revealed it unto thee, but my Father which is in heaven.* Here it is plainly intimated that a belief of Jesus being the Christ, the Son of the living God, is saving faith; and that no man can be strictly said to do this, unless he be the subject of a spiritual illumination from above. To the same purpose are those express declarations of Paul and John: – *If thou shalt confess with thy mouth the Lord Jesus, and shalt believe in thine heart that God hath raised him from the dead, thou shalt be saved. – Whosoever shall confess that Jesus is the Son of God, God dwelleth in him, and he in God. – Whosoever believeth that Jesus is the Christ is born of God. – Who is he that overcometh the world, but he that believeth that Jesus is the Son of God? – He that hath received his testimony hath set to his seal that God is true. – No man can say that Jesus is the Lord, but by the Holy Ghost.* – Again, *While ye have the light, believe in the light, that ye may be the children of light.* The *light* they then had was that of the Gospel; and had they believed it, they would have been the children of light, or true Christians. *Ye sent unto John, and he bare witness unto the truth ... These things I say, that ye might be saved.* Our Lord could not mean less, by this language, than that, if they believed those things which John testified, and which he himself confirmed, they would be saved; which is the same thing as declaring it to be saving faith. *Christ shall come to be glorified in his saints, and to be admired in all them that believe (because our testimony among you was believed) in that day.* The words in a parenthesis are evidently intended to give the reason of the phrase *them that believe,* and intimate that it was the belief of the Gospel testimony that denominated them believers. *God hath chosen us to salvation through sanctification of the Spirit and belief of the truth.* It cannot be doubted, that, by the *belief of the truth,* is here meant faith in Christ; and its being connected with sanctification of the Spirit, and eternal salvation, proves it to be saving. (*Mark 16:16; John 20:31; Luke 8:12; Matthew 16:16, 17; Romans 10:9; 1 John 4:15; 5:1, 5; John 3:33; 1 Corinthians 12:3; John 12:36; 5:33, 34; 2 Thessalonians 1:10; 2:13*).

If the foregoing passages be admitted to prove the point, (and if they do not, we may despair of learning anything from the Scriptures,) the duty of unconverted sinners to believe in Christ cannot fairly be called in question; for, as before said, it is admitted on all hands that it is the duty of every man to believe what God reveals.

But to this statement it is objected that Christianity having at that time great opposition made to it, and its professors being consequently exposed to great persecution and reproach, the belief and acknowledgment of the Gospel was more a test of sincerity than it now is. Men are now taught the principles of the Christian religion from their youth, and believe them, and are not ashamed to acknowledge them, while yet they give no evidence of their being born of God, but of the contrary. There is some force in this objection, so far as it respects *the confession* of Christ's name; but I do not perceive that it affects the belief of the Gospel. It was no more difficult to believe the truth at that time than at this, though it might be much more so to avow it. With respect to that traditional assent which is given to Christianity in some nations, it is of the same nature as that which is given to Mohammedanism and Paganism in others. It is no more than that of the Jewish nation, in the time of our Lord, towards the Mosaic Scriptures. They declared themselves to be Moses' disciples, and had no doubt that they believed him; yet our Lord did not allow that they believed his writings. *Had ye believed Moses*, says he, *ye would have believed me; for he wrote of me. (John 5:46)*. The same is doubtless true of all others who assent to his Gospel, merely from having been educated in it. If they did believe it, they would be consistent, and embrace those things which are connected with it. It is worthy of remark, that those professors of Christianity who *received not the love of the truth, that they might be saved*, are represented as *not believing the truth*, and as having *pleasure in unrighteousness. (2 Thessalonians 2:10, 12)*. To admit the existence of a few facts, without possessing any sense of their humiliating implication, their holy nature, their vast importance, or the practical consequences that attach to them, is to admit the body without the spirit. Paul, notwithstanding his knowledge of the law, and great zeal on its behalf, while blind to its *spirituality*, reckoned himself to be *without the law, (Romans 7:9)*. And such are those professing Christians, with respect to the Gospel, *who receive not the love of the truth, that they may be saved.*

It is further objected, that men are said to have believed the Gospel, who, notwithstanding, were destitute of true religion. Thus, some among the chief rulers are said to have *believed Jesus, but did not confess him; for they loved the praise of men more than the praise of God. (John 12:42, 43)*. It is said of Simon, that he *believed also;* yet he was *in the gall of bitterness, and in the bond of iniquity.* Agrippa is acknowledged by Paul to have believed the prophets; and faith is attributed even to the devils. The term *belief*, like almost every other term, is sometimes used in an improper sense. Judas is said to have *repented*, and hanged himself; though nothing more is meant by it than his being smitten with remorse, wishing he had not done as he did, on account of the consequences. Through the poverty of language, there is not a name for everything that differs; and, therefore, where two things have the same visible appearance, and differ only in some circumstances which are invisible, it is common to call them by the same name. Thus men are termed *honest* who are punctual in their dealings, though such conduct, in many instances, may arise merely from a regard to their own credit, interest, or safety. Thus the remorse of Judas is called *repentance;* and thus the convictions of the Jewish rulers, of Simon, and Agrippa, and the fearful apprehension of apostate angels, from what they had already felt, is called *faith*. But as we do not infer from the application of the term *repentance* to the feelings of Judas, that there is nothing spiritual in *real* repentance, so neither ought we to conclude, from the foregoing applications of the term *believing*, that there is nothing spiritual in a *real* belief of the Gospel.

"The objects of faith," it has been said, "are not bare axioms or propositions. The act of the believer does not terminate at an axiom, but at *the thing;* for axioms are not formed, but that, by them, knowledge may be had of *things*." To believe a bare axiom or proposition, in distinction from the thing, must be barely to believe that such and such letters make certain words; and that such words, put together, have a certain meaning: but who would call this believing the proposition? To believe the proposition, is to believe *the thing*. Letters, syllables, words, and propositions, are only means of conveyance; and these, as such, are not the objects of faith, but the *thing conveyed*. Nevertheless, those things must have a conveyance, so that they can be believed in. The *person, blood*, and *righteousness of Christ*, for instance, are often said to be objects of faith; and this they doubtless are, as they are objects held forth to us by the language of Scripture: but they could not meet our faith, unless something were *affirmed concerning them* in letters and syllables, or vocal sounds, or by some means or other of conveyance. To say, therefore, that these are objects of faith, is to say the truth, but not the whole truth. The person, blood, and righteousness of Christ, *revealed in the Scriptures as the way of a sinner's acceptance with God*, are, properly speaking, the objects of our faith; for without such a revelation, it would be impossible to believe in them.

Some writers have considered faith in Christ as a *dependence* on him, a *receiving* him, a *coming* to him, and *trusting in him* for salvation. There is no doubt but these terms are frequently used, in the New Testament, to express believing. "As many as *received* him, to them gave he power to become the sons of God, even to them that believe on his name." – "He that *cometh* to me shall never hunger; and he that *believeth* on me shall never thirst." – "That we should be to the praise of his glory, who first *trusted* in Christ." – "I know whom I have *believed*, and am persuaded that he is able to keep that which I have *committed unto him* against that day." (*John 1:12; 6:35; Ephesians 1:12; 2 Timothy 1:12*). Whether these terms, however, strictly speaking, convey the same idea as believing, may admit of a question. They seem, rather, to be the immediate effects of faith, than faith itself. The author of the *Epistle to the Hebrews* describes the order of these things, in what he says of the faith of Enoch: – *He that cometh to God must believe that he is, and that he is a rewarder of them that diligently seek him. (Hebrews 11:6).* Here are three different exercises of mind: *First*, believing *that God is; second*, believing that he is *a rewarder of them that diligently seek him; third, coming* to him: and the last is represented as the effect of the former two. The same may be applied to Christ. He that cometh to Christ must believe the Gospel testimony, that he is the Son of God, and the Saviour of sinners – the only name given under heaven, and among men, by which we must be saved. He must also believe the Gospel promise, that he will bestow eternal salvation on all them that obey him; and under the influence of this persuasion, he *comes* to him, *commits* himself to him, or *trusts* the salvation of his soul into his hands. This process may be so quick as not to admit of the mind being conscious of it; and especially as, at such a time, it is otherwise employed than in speculating upon its own operations. So far as it is able to recollect, the whole may appear to be one complex exercise of the soul. In this large sense, also, as comprehending not only the credit of the Gospel testimony, but the soul's dependence on Christ alone for acceptance with God, it is allowed that believing is necessary, not only to salvation, but to justification. We must come to Jesus, that we may have *life*. Those who attain the blessing of justification, must *seek it by faith*, and *not by the works of the law – submitting* themselves to the righteousness of God. This blessing is constantly represented as following our union with Christ: and *he that is joined to the Lord is one spirit. (John 5:40; Romans 9:31, 32; 10:3; 1 Corinthians 6:17).*

Let it but be granted that a real belief of the Gospel is not merely a matter presupposed in saving faith, but that it enters into the essence of it, and the writer of these pages will be far from contending for the exclusion of trust or dependence.

The term *trust* appears to be most appropriate, or best adapted of any, to express the confidence which the soul reposes in Christ for the fulfilment of his *promises*. We may credit a report of evil tidings as well as one of good; but we cannot be said to trust it. We may also credit a report, the truth or falsehood of which does not at all *concern* us; but that in which we place *trust* must be something in which our well-being is involved. The relinquishment of false confidences which the Gospel requires, and the risk which is made in embracing it, are likewise better expressed by this term than by any other. A true belief of the record which God has given of his Son, is accompanied with all this; but the term *belief* does not, of itself, necessarily convey it. When Jacob's sons brought the coat of many colours to him, he credited their story; he believed Joseph to be torn in pieces; but he could not be said to *trust* that he was. When the same persons, on their return from Egypt, declared that Joseph was yet alive, Jacob, at first, believed them not. But, on seeing the wagons, he was satisfied of the truth of their declaration, and *trusted* in it too – leaving all behind him because of it.

But, whatever difference there may be between *credit* and *trust*, they agree in those particulars which affect the point at issue: the one, no less than the other, has relation to *revealed truth* as its foundation. In some cases, it directly refers to the divine veracity, as in *Psalm 119:42*, "*I trust in thy word.*" And where the immediate reference is to the power, the wisdom, or the mercy of God, or to the righteousness of Christ, there is a remote relation to veracity; for neither the one nor the other would be objects of trust, were they not revealed in a way of *promise*. And from hence it will follow, that, trusting in Christ, no less than crediting his testimony, is the duty of every sinner to whom the revelation is made.

If it be asked, What ground could a sinner who shall, at last, prove to have no interest in the salvation of Christ, ever possess for trusting in him? let it be considered what it was for which he was warranted or obliged to trust. Was it that Christ would save him, whether he believed in him or not? No – there is no such promise; but an explicit declaration of the contrary. To trust in this, therefore, would be to trust in a falsehood. That for which he ought to have trusted in him was, the obtaining of mercy, *in case he applied for it*. For this there was a complete warrant in the Gospel declarations. I may add, if any man distrust either the power or willingness of Christ to save those that come to him, and so continue to stand at a distance, relying upon his own righteousness, or some false ground of confidence, to the rejection of him, it is criminal and inexcusable unbelief.

2

Faith in Christ – the Duty of All who Hear the Gospel

WHAT has been already advanced on the nature of faith in Christ, may contribute to the deciding of the question, Whether faith be the duty of the ungodly; but, in addition to this, the Scriptures furnish abundance of positive evidence. The principal part of that which has occurred to me, may be comprehended under the following propositions: –

I. UNCONVERTED SINNERS ARE COMMANDED, EXHORTED, AND INVITED TO BELIEVE IN CHRIST FOR SALVATION.

It is here taken for granted, that whatever God commands, exhorts, or invites us to comply with, is the duty of those to whom such language is addressed. If, therefore, saving faith be not the duty of the unconverted, we may expect never to find any addresses of this nature directed to them in the Holy Scriptures. We may expect that God will as soon require them to become angels as Christians, if the one be no more their duty than the other.

There is a phraseology suited to different periods of time. Prior to the coming of Christ, and the preaching of the Gospel, we read but little of believing; but other terms, fully expressive of the thing, are found in abundance. I shall select a few examples, and accompany them with such remarks as may show them to be applicable to the subject.

Psalm 2:11, 12. – Serve the Lord with fear, and rejoice with trem-
bling. Kiss the Son, lest he be angry, and ye perish from the way,
when his wrath is kindled but a little. Blessed are all they that put
their trust in him.

The psalm is evidently a prophecy of the resurrection and exalta-
tion of the Messiah. Whatever reference may be had to Solomon,
there are several things which are not true, of either him or his government; and the whole is applicable to Christ, and is plentifully
applied to him in the New Testament.

The *kings and judges of the earth*, who are here admonished to
serve the Lord Messiah with fear, and to *kiss the Son, lest he be angry*,
are the same persons mentioned in *verse 2*, which words we find, in
the New Testament, applied to *Herod and Pontius Pilate, with the*
Gentiles, and the people of Israel, (*Acts 4:27*): that is, they were the
enemies of Christ, unregenerate sinners; and such, for anything that
appears, they lived and died.

The command of God addressed to these rulers, is of a *spiritual*
nature, including unfeigned faith in the Messiah, and sincere obedience to his authority. To *kiss the Son*, is to be reconciled to him, to
embrace his Word and ordinances, and bow to his sceptre. To *serve*
him with fear, and rejoice with trembling, denote that they should not
think meanly of him, on the one hand; nor hypocritically cringe to
him, from a mere apprehension of his wrath, on the other; but sincerely embrace his government, and even *rejoice* that they had it to
embrace. That which is here required of unbelievers, is the very spirit
which distinguishes believers; a holy fear of Christ's majesty, and a
humble confidence in his mercy; taking his yoke upon them, and
wearing it as their highest delight. That the object of the command
was spiritual, is also manifest from the threatening and the promise
annexed to it, *lest ye perish from the way ... blessed are all they that put*
their trust in him. It is here plainly supposed that, if they did embrace
the Son, they should not perish from the way, and, if they did put
their trust in him, they should be blessed. The result is – Unconverted
sinners are commanded to believe in Christ for salvation: therefore,
believing in Christ for salvation is their duty.

Isaiah 55:1-7. – Ho, every one that thirsteth, come ye to the waters,
and he that hath no money; come ye, buy, and eat; yea, come, buy

wine and milk without money and without price. Wherefore do ye spend money for that which is not bread? and your labour for that which satisfieth not? Hearken diligently unto me, and eat ye that which is good, and let your soul delight itself in fatness. Incline your ear, and come unto me: hear, and your soul shall live; and I will make an everlasting covenant with you, even the sure mercies of David. Behold, I have given him for a witness to the people, a leader and commander to the people. Behold, thou shalt call a nation that thou knowest not, and nations that knew not thee shall run unto thee because of the Lord thy God, and for the Holy One of Israel; for he hath glorified thee. Seek ye the Lord while he may be found, call ye upon him while he is near: let the wicked forsake his way, and the unrighteous man his thoughts: and let him return unto the Lord, and he will have mercy upon him; and to our God, for he will abundantly pardon.

This is the language of invitation: but divine invitation implies an obligation to accept it; otherwise, the conduct of those who *made light* of the Gospel supper, and preferred their farms and merchandise before it, would have been guiltless.

The concluding verses of this passage express those things literally, which the foregoing ones described metaphorically: the persons invited, and the invitation, are the same in both. The *thirst* which they are supposed to possess, does not mean a holy desire after spiritual blessings, but the natural desire of happiness which God has implanted in every bosom; and which, in wicked men, is directed, not to *the sure mercies of David*, but to that which *is not bread*, or which has no solid satisfaction in it. The *duty*, to a compliance with which they are so feelingfully urged, is a relinquishment of every false way, and a returning to God in the name of him who was given for *a witness, a leader and a commander to the people;* which is the same thing as *repentance towards God, and faith towards our Lord Jesus Christ.* The encouragements held up to induce a compliance with this duty are the freeness, the substantialness, the durability, the certainty, and the rich abundance of those blessings, which as many as repent and believe the Gospel shall receive. The whole passage is exceedingly explicit, as to the duty of the unconverted; neither is it possible to evade the force of it by any just or fair method of interpretation.

Jeremiah 6:16. Thus saith the Lord, Stand ye in the ways, and see, and ask for the old paths, where is the good way, and walk therein, and ye shall find rest for your souls. But they said, We will not walk therein.

The people here addressed are, beyond all doubt, ungodly men. God himself bears witness of them, that *their ears were uncircumcised, and they could not hearken, for the word of the Lord was to them a reproach, and they had no delight in it,* (*verse 10*). Yea, so hardened were they, that *they were not ashamed when they had committed abomination,* and so impudent, that *they could not blush,* (*verse 15*). And such, for anything that appears, they continued; for when they were exhorted to *walk in the good way,* their answer was, *We will not walk therein.* Hence the awful threatening which follows: *Hear, O earth: behold, I will bring evil upon this people, even the fruit of their thoughts, because they have not hearkened unto my words, nor to my law, but rejected it,* (*verse 19*).

The *good way,* in which they were directed to walk, must have been the same as that in which the patriarchs and prophets had walked in former ages; who, we all know, lived and died in the faith of the promised Messiah. Hence, our Lord, with great propriety, applied the passage to himself, (*Matthew 11:28, 29*). Jeremiah directed to the old paths, and the good way, as the only medium of finding rest to the soul: Jesus said, *Come unto* ME, *all ye that labour·and are heavy laden, and I will give you rest. Take my yoke upon you, and learn of me; for I am meek and lowly in heart: and ye shall find rest unto your souls.*

We see in this passage also, as in many others, in what manner God requires sinners to *use the means of grace;* not by a mere attendance upon them, (which, while the end is disregarded, and the means rested in instead of it, is not using, but perverting them,) but with a sincere desire to find out the good way, and to walk in it. God requires no natural impossibilities. No man is required to believe in Christ, before he has opportunity of examining the evidence attending his Gospel: but he ought to search into it, like the noble Bereans, immediately, and with a pure intention of finding and following the good way; which, if he do, like them he will soon be found walking in it. If we teach sinners that a mere attendance on the means of grace is that use of them which God requires at their hands, and in which consists the whole of their duty, as to repentance towards God, and faith towards our Lord Jesus Christ, we shall be found false witnesses for God, and deceivers of the souls of men.

The New Testament is still more explicit than the Old. Faith in Jesus Christ, even that which is accompanied with salvation, is there constantly held up as the duty of all to whom the Gospel is preached.

John 12:36. – While ye have the light, believe in the light, that ye may be the children of light.

The persons to whom this passage was addressed, were unbelievers; such who, *though Jesus had done so many miracles among them, yet believed not on him, (verse 37)*: and it appears that they continued unbelievers, for they are represented as given over to judicial blindness and hardness of heart, *(verse 40)*. The *light* which they were exhorted to believe in, appears to be himself, as revealed in the Gospel; for thus he speaks in the context, *I am come a light into the world, that whosoever believeth on me should not abide in darkness. (verse 46)*. And that the believing which Christ required of them was such as, had it been complied with, would have issued in their salvation, is manifest, from its being added, *that ye may be the children of light;* an appellation never bestowed on any but true believers.

John 6:29. – This is the work of God, that ye believe on him whom he hath sent.

These words contain an answer to a question. The persons who asked it were men who *followed Christ for loaves,* who *believed not,* and who, after this, *walked no more with him, (verses 26, 36, 66).* Christ had been rebuking them for their mercenary principles in thus following him about, and charging them, saying, *Labour not for the meat which perisheth, but for that meat which endureth unto everlasting life, (verse 27).* They replied by asking, *What shall we do, that we might work the works of God?* which was saying, in effect, 'We have been very zealous for thee in following thee hither and thither: yet thou dost not allow that we please God: thou directest us to *labour for that meat which endureth unto everlasting life.* What wouldest thou have us do? what can we do? what must we do, in order to please God?' To this question our Lord answers, *This is the work of God, that ye believe on him whom he hath sent;* which, if it be a proper answer, is the same as saying, This is the first and greatest of all duties; and, without it, no other duty can be acceptable.

It has been said, in answer to the argument from this passage, "The words contain a declaration, that believing in Christ for salvation is necessary to the enjoyment of eternal life, and that faith in him is an act acceptable and pleasing to God; but they afford no proof, that it is required of men in a state of unregeneracy. To declare to unregenerate people the necessity of faith, in order to salvation, which is what our blessed Lord here does, falls very far short of asserting it to be their present duty."

We see, by this answer, that Mr Brine, who will be allowed to have been one of the most judicious writers on that side of the question, was fully convinced of three things. *First:* That the persons here addressed were unregenerate sinners. *Second:* That the faith recommended is saving. *Third:* That, when faith is called the *work of God,* it does not mean the work which God *performs,* but an act of theirs, which would be *acceptable* and *pleasing* to him. Yet we are told, that our Lord merely expresses the *necessity* of it, without asserting it to be their present *duty.* Was it not the object of their inquiry, then, What was their present duty? or, What they ought to do, in order to please God? What else can be made of it? Further: how can our Lord be supposed, in answer to their question, to tell them of an act which was necessary, acceptable, and pleasing to God, but which was not their present duty? Is such an answer worthy of him? Nay, how could their believing be an act acceptable and pleasing to God, if it were not their present duty? God is pleased with that only in us which he requires at our hands.

John 5:22, 23. – The Father hath committed all judgment unto the Son: that all men should honour the Son, even as they honour the Father. He that honoureth not the Son honoureth not the Father which hath sent him.

That men are obliged to honour the Father by a holy, hearty love to him, and adoration of him, under every character by which he has manifested himself, will be allowed by all, except the grossest Antinomians; and, if it is the will of the Father that all men should honour the Son, even as they honour the Father, nothing less can be required of them than a holy, hearty love to him, and adoration of him, under every character by which he has manifested himself. But such a regard to Christ necessarily supposes faith in him; for it is impossible to honour him while we reject him in all or any of his offices, and neglect his great salvation. To honour an infallible teacher, is to place an implicit and unbounded confidence in all he says: to honour an advocate, is to commit our cause to him: to honour a physician, is to trust our lives in his hands: and to honour a king, is to bow to his sceptre, and cheerfully obey his laws. These are characters under which Christ has manifested himself. To treat him in this manner, is to honour him; and to treat him otherwise, is to dishonour him.

The Scriptures, both of the Old and New Testament, abound with exhortations to hear the word of God, to *hearken* to his counsel, to wait on him, to seek his favour, etc, all which imply saving faith.

> HEARKEN *unto me, O ye children: for blessed are they that keep my ways.* HEAR *instruction, and be wise, and refuse it not. Blessed is the man that* HEARETH *me, watching daily at my gates, waiting at the posts of my doors. For whoso findeth me findeth life, and shall obtain favour of the Lord. But he that sinneth against me, wrongeth his own soul: all they that hate me love death.* − *How long, ye simple ones, will ye love simplicity? and the scorners delight in their scorning, and fools hate knowledge?* TURN *you at my reproof: behold, I will pour out my Spirit unto you, I will make known my words unto you.* − HEAR, *ye deaf; and look, ye blind, that ye may see.* − HEARKEN *diligently unto me.* − INCLINE *your ear, and come unto me:* HEAR, *and your soul shall live.* − SEEK *ye the Lord while he may be found,* CALL YE UPON HIM *while he is near.* − *This is my beloved Son:* HEAR *him.* − *And it shall come to pass, that every soul, which will not* HEAR *that prophet, shall be destroyed from among the people.* − LABOUR *not for the meat that perisheth, but for that meat which endureth unto everlasting life.* (Proverbs 8:32-36; 1:22, 23; Isaiah 42:18; 55:2, 3, 6; Mark 9:7; Acts 3:23; John 6:27).*

It is a grievous misapplication of such language to consider it as expressive of a mere attendance upon the means of grace, without any spiritual desire after God; and to allow that unregenerate sinners comply with it. Nothing can be further from the truth.

The Scriptures abound in promises of spiritual and eternal blessings to those who thus *hearken, hear,* and *seek* after God. Such exercises, therefore, must, of necessity, be spiritual, and require to be understood as including faith in Christ. The Scriptures exhort to no such exercises as may be complied with by a mind at enmity with God. The duties which they inculcate are all spiritual; and no sinner, while unregenerate, is supposed to comply with them. So far from allowing that ungodly men *seek* after God, or do any *good thing*, they expressly declare the contrary. "God looked down from heaven upon the children of men, to see if there were any that did *understand*, that did *seek* God. Every one of them is gone back: they are altogether become filthy; there is none that *doeth good*, no, not one." (*Psalm 53:2, 3*). To reduce the exhortations of Scripture to the level of a carnal mind, is to betray the authority of God over the human heart; and to allow that unconverted sinners comply with them, is to be aiding and abetting in their self-deception. The unconverted who attend the means of grace, generally persuade themselves, and wish to persuade others, that they would gladly be converted, and be real Christians, if it were but in their power. They imagine themselves to be waiting at the pool for the moving of the water, and therefore feel no guilt on account of their present state of mind. Doubtless they are willing and desirous to escape the wrath to come, and, under certain convictions, would submit to relinquish many things, and to comply with other things, as the condition of it; but they have no direct desire after spiritual blessings. If they had, they would seek them in the name of Jesus, and, thus seeking, would find them. That preaching, therefore, which exhorts them to mere outward duties, and tells them that their only concern is in this manner to wait at the pool, helps forward their delusion, and, should they perish, will prove accessary to their destruction.

Simon the sorcerer was admonished to *repent, and pray to the Lord, if perhaps the thought of his heart might be forgiven him*. From this express example, many, who are averse from the doctrine here defended, have been so far convinced as to acknowledge that it is the duty of the unconverted to pray, at least for temporal blessings; but Simon was not admonished to pray for temporal blessings, but for *the forgiveness of sin*. Neither was he to pray in a carnal and heartless manner; but to *repent*, and pray. And, being directed to *repent*, and pray for the *forgiveness of sin*, he was, in effect, directed to believe in Jesus; for in what other name could forgiveness be expected? Peter, after having declared to the Jewish rulers that *there was none other name under heaven given among men, whereby we must be saved*, cannot be supposed to have directed Simon to hope for forgiveness in any other way.

To admonish any person to pray, or to seek the divine favour, in any other way than by *faith in Jesus Christ*, is the same thing as to admonish him to follow the example of Cain, and of the self-righteous Jews. Cain was not averse from worship. He brought his offering; but having no sense of the evil of sin, and of the need of a Saviour, he had taken no notice of what had been revealed concerning the promised Seed, and paid no regard to the presenting of an expiatory sacrifice. He thanked God for temporal blessings, and might pray for their continuance; but this was not *doing well*. It was practically saying to his Maker, 'I have done nothing to deserve being made a sacrifice to thy displeasure, and I see no necessity for any sacrifice being offered up, either now or at the end of the world.' In short, it was claiming to approach God merely as a creature, and as though nothing had taken place which required an atonement. The self-righteous Jews did not live without religion; they followed after the law of righteousness; yet they did not attain it; and wherefore? *Because they sought it not by faith, but as it were by the works of the law. For they stumbled at that stumbling-stone. (Romans 9:32).* And shall we direct our hearers to follow this example, by exhorting them to pray, and seek the divine favour, in any other way than by faith in Jesus Christ? If so, how can we deserve the name of Christian ministers?

The Scriptures exhort sinners to put their *trust* in the Lord, and censure them for placing it in an arm of flesh. Whether trusting in Christ for the salvation of our souls be distinguishable from believing in him or not, it certainly includes it. To trust in Christ is to believe in him. If, therefore, the one be required, the other must be. Those who *loved vanity, and sought after leasing*, are admonished to *offer the sacrifices of righteousness,* and to *put their trust in the Lord, Psalm 4:2, 5;* and a trust connected with the sacrifices of righteousness must be spiritual. To rely on any other object is to *trust in vanity*, against which sinners are repeatedly warned.

Trust not in oppression, and become not vain in robbery. – He that trusteth in his own heart is a fool. – Cursed be the man that trusteth in man, and maketh flesh his arm, and whose heart departeth from the Lord. (Psalm 62:10; Proverbs 28:26; Jeremiah 17:5).

It is allowed, that, if God had never sent his Son into the world to save sinners, or if the invitations of the Gospel were not addressed to sinners indefinitely, there would be no warrant for trust in the divine mercy; and as it is, there is no warrant for trust beyond what God has promised in his Word. He has not promised to save sinners indiscriminately; and therefore it would be presumption in sinners indiscriminately to trust that they shall be saved. But he has promised, and that in great variety of language, that *whosoever, relinquishing every false ground of hope, shall come to Jesus as a perishing sinner, and rely on him alone for salvation, shall not be disappointed.* For such a reliance, therefore, there is a complete warrant. These promises are true, and will be fulfilled, whether we trust in them or not; and whoso still continues to trust in his own righteousness, or in the general mercy of his Creator, without respect to the atonement, refusing to build upon the foundation which God has laid in Zion, is guilty of the greatest of all sins; and if God give him not repentance to the acknowledgment of the truth, the stone which he has refused will fall upon him, and grind him to powder.

But "until a man, through the law, is dead to the law," says Mr Brine, "he hath no *warrant* to receive Christ as a Saviour, or to hope for salvation through him." [1] If, by receiving Christ, were meant the *claiming an interest in the blessings of his salvation*, this objection would be well founded. No man, while adhering to his own righteousness as the ground of acceptance with God, has any warrant to conclude himself interested in the righteousness of Jesus. The Scriptures everywhere assure him of the contrary. But the question is, Does he need any warrant to be *dead to the law?* or, which is the same thing, to relinquish his vain hopes of acceptance by the works of it, and to choose that Rock for his foundation which is chosen of God and precious? To "receive" Christ, in the sense of Scripture, stands opposed to *rejecting* him, or to such a non-reception of him as was practised by the body of the Jewish nation. (*John 1:11, 12*).

---

1. *Motives to Love and Unity*, pages 38, 39.

An interest in spiritual blessings, and, of course, a persuasion of it, is represented as following the reception of Christ, and, consequently, is to be distinguished from it: *To as many as received him, to them gave he power to become the sons of God, even to them that believe on his name.* The idea that is generally attached to the term, in various cases to which the reception of Christ bears an allusion, corresponds with the above statement. To receive a *gift*, is not to believe it to be my own, though, after I have received it, it is so, but to have my pride so far abased as not to be above it, and my heart so much attracted as to be willing to relinquish everything that stands in competition with it. To receive a *guest*, is not to believe him to be my particular friend, though such he may be, but to open my doors to him, and make him heartily welcome. To receive an *instructor*, is not to believe him to be my instructor any more than another's, but to embrace his instruction, and follow his counsel. For a town or city, after a long siege, to receive a *king*, is not to believe him to be their special friend, though such he may be, and, in the end, they may see it, but to lay down their arms, throw open their gates, and come under his government. These remarks are easily applied; and it is no less easy to perceive that every sinner has not only a warrant thus to receive Christ, but that it is his great sin if he receive him not.

II. EVERY MAN IS BOUND CORDIALLY TO RECEIVE AND APPROVE WHATEVER GOD REVEALS.

It may be presumed, that, if God reveals anything to men, it will be accompanied with such evidence of its being what it is, that no upright man can continue to doubt of it: *He that is of God heareth God's words. (John 8:47).*

It will be allowed, by those with whom I am now reasoning, that no man is justifiable in disbelieving the truth of the Gospel, or in positively rejecting it; but then it is supposed that a belief of the Gospel is not saving faith, and that, though a positive rejection of divine truth is sinful, yet a spiritual reception of it is not a duty. I hope it has been made clear, in the first chapter, that a real belief of the doctrine of Christ is saving faith, and includes such a cordial acquiescence in the way of salvation as has the promise of eternal life. But, be this as it may, whether the belief of the Gospel be allowed to include a cordial acquiescence in God's way of salvation or not, such an acquiescence will be allowed to include saving faith. If, therefore, it can be proved that a cordial approbation of God's way of saving sinners is the duty of everyone, it will amount to proving the same thing of saving faith.

I allow there is a difficulty in this part of the work; but it is that which attends the proof of a truth which is nearly self-evident. Ought we not, if we think of Christ at all, to think *suitably* of him? and are we justifiable in entertaining low and unsuitable thoughts of him? Is it not a matter of *complaint* that the ungodly Jews *saw no form nor comeliness in him, nor beauty that they should desire him?* And with respect to a *hearty choice* of him, as God's appointed way of salvation, if it be not the duty of sinners to choose him, it is their duty to refuse him, or to desire to be accepted of God by the works of their hands, in preference to him. But how can we complain of sinners for their not choosing Christ, if they be under no obligation to do so? Is there no sin in the invention of the various false schemes of religion with which the Christian world abounds, to the exclusion of Christ? Why, then, are heresies reckoned among *the works of the flesh?* (*Galatians 5:20*). If we are not obliged to think suitably of Christ, and to choose him whom the Lord and all good men have chosen, there can be no evil in these things; for where no law is, there is no transgression.

A hearty choice of God's appointed way of salvation, is the same thing as falling in with its grand designs. Now, the grand designs of the salvation of Christ are, *the glory of God, the abasement of the sinner,* and *the destruction of his sins.* It is God's manifest purpose, in saving sinners, to save them in this way; and can any sinner be excused from cordially acquiescing in it? If any man properly regards the character of God, he must be willing that he should be glorified: if he knew his own unworthiness as he ought to know it, he must also be willing to occupy that place which the Gospel way of salvation assigns him: and if he be not wickedly wedded to his lusts, he must be willing to sacrifice them at the foot of the cross. He may be averse from each of these, and, while an unbeliever, is so; but he will not be able to acquit himself of guilt; and it is to be lamented that any who sustain the character of Christian ministers should be employed in labouring to acquit him.

If a way of salvation were provided which did *not* provide for the glory of God, which did *not* abase, but flatter the sinner, and which did *not* require him to sacrifice his lusts, he would feel no want of power to embrace it. Nominal Christians, and mere professors, in all ages, have shown themselves able to believe anything but the truth. Thus it was with the carnal Jews, and thus our Lord plainly told them:

I am come in my Father's name, and ye receive me not: if another shall come in his own name, him ye will receive. – Because I tell you the truth, ye believe me not. Which of you convinceth me of sin? And if I say the truth, why do ye not believe me? He that is of God heareth God's words: ye therefore hear them not, because ye are not of God. (John 5:43; 8:45-47).

This is the true source of the innumerable false schemes of religion in the world, and the true reason why the Gospel is not universally embraced.

Unbelievers are described as disallowing him who is *chosen of God, and precious. (1 Peter 2:4-7).* Now, either to allow or disallow supposes a claim. Christ claims to be the whole foundation of a sinner's hope; and God claims, on his behalf, that he be treated as *the head of the corner.* But the heart of unbelievers cannot allow the claim. The Jewish builders set him at nought; and every self-righteous heart follows their example. God, to express his displeasure at this conduct, assures them that their unbelief shall affect none but themselves. It shall not deprive the Saviour of his honours; *for the stone which they refuse,* notwithstanding their opposition, *shall become the head of the corner.* What can be made of all this, but that they ought to have allowed him the place which he so justly claimed, and to have chosen him whom the Lord had chosen? On no other ground could the Scripture censure them as it does, and on no other principle could they be characterised as *disobedient;* for all disobedience consists in a breach of duty.

Believers, on the other hand, are described as thinking highly of Christ; reckoning themselves unworthy to *unloose the latchet of his shoes,* or that he should *come under their roof;* treating his Gospel as *worthy of all acceptation,* and *counting all things but loss for the excellency of the knowledge of him.* They are of the same mind with the blessed above, who sing his praise, *saying with a loud voice*, WORTHY *is the Lamb that was slain to receive power, and riches, and wisdom, and strength, and honour, and glory, and blessing.* In summary, they are of the same mind with God himself. Him whom God has chosen, they choose; and he that is *precious* in his sight, is *precious* in theirs. (*Mark 1:7; 1 Timothy 1:15; Philippians 3:8; Revelation 5:12; 1 Peter 2:4-7*). And do they overestimate his character? Is he not worthy of all the honour they ascribe to him; of all the affection they exercise towards him; and that, whether they actually receive it or not? If all the angels had been of the mind of Satan, and all the saints of the spirit of the unbelieving Israelites who were not gathered, yet would he have been *glorious in the eyes of the Lord.* The belief or unbelief of creatures, makes no difference as to his worthiness, or their obligation to ascribe it to him.

It is allowed by all, except the grossest Antinomians, that every man is obliged to love God with all his heart, soul, mind, and strength; and this, notwithstanding the depravity of his nature. But to love God with all the heart, is to love him *in every character in which he has made himself known, and more especially in those wherein his moral excellences appear with the brightest lustre.* The same law that obliged Adam, in innocence, to love God in all his perfections, as displayed in the works of creation, obliged Moses and Israel to love him in all the glorious displays of himself in his wonderful works of providence of which they were witnesses. And the same law that obliged them to love him in those discoveries of himself, obliges us to love him in other discoveries, by which he has since more gloriously appeared, as *saving sinners through the death of his Son.* To suppose that we are obliged to love God as manifesting himself in the works of creation and providence, but not in the work of redemption, is to suppose that, in the highest and most glorious display of himself, he deserves no regard. The same perfections which appear in all his other works, and render him lovely, appear in this with a ten-fold lustre. To be obliged to love him on account of the one, and not of the other, is not a little extraordinary.

As these things cannot be separated in point of obligation, so neither can they *in fact.* He that loves God for any excellency, as manifested in one form, must, of necessity, love him for that excellency, let it be manifested in what form it may; and the brighter the display, the stronger will be his love. This remark is verified in the holy angels. At first, they loved their Maker, for what they saw in his works of creation. They saw him lay the foundation of the earth, and they SHOUTED FOR JOY. In process of time, they witnessed the glorious displays of his moral character in the government of the world which he had made; and now their love increases. On every new occasion, they cry, HOLY, HOLY, HOLY IS THE LORD OF HOSTS: THE WHOLE EARTH IS FULL OF HIS GLORY. At length, they beheld an event, to the accomplishment of which all former events were subservient; they saw the Messiah born in Bethlehem. And now their love rises still higher. As though heaven could not contain them on such an occasion, they gather at the place, and contemplate the good that should arise to the moral system, bursting forth into a song: GLORY TO GOD IN THE HIGHEST, AND ON EARTH PEACE, GOOD WILL TOWARDS MEN. All this was but the natural operation of love to God; and, from the same principle, they took delight in attending the Redeemer through his life, strengthening him in his sufferings, watching at his tomb, conducting him to glory, and *looking into* the mysteries of redemption. With a heart like theirs, is it possible to conceive that we should continue impenitent or unbelieving? If, in our circumstances, we possessed that love to God by which they were influenced, it would melt us into holy lamentation for having sinned against him. If the gospel invitation to partake of the water of life once sounded in our ears, we should instantly imbibe it. Instead of making *light of it*, and preferring our *farms* and our *merchandise* before it, we should embrace it with our whole heart. Let any creature be affected towards God as the holy angels are, and if he had a thousand souls to be saved, and the invitation extended to everyone that is willing, he would not hesitate a moment, whether he should rely on his salvation. It is owing to a want of love to God, that any man continues impenitent or unbelieving. This was plainly intimated by our Lord to the Jews: *I know you, that ye have not the love of God in you. I am come in my Father's name, and ye receive me not. (John 5:42, 43).* It is impossible to love God, and not to embrace the greatest friend of God that ever existed; or to love his law, and not approve of a system which, above all things, tends to magnify and make it honourable.

"The affections included in divine love," says an able writer, "are founded on those truths for which there is the greatest evidence in the world. Everything in the world that proves the being of God, proves that his creatures should love him with all their hearts. The evidence for these things is, in *itself* very strong, and level to every capacity. Where it does not beget conviction, it is not owing to the weakness of men's capacities, but the strength of their prejudices and prepossessions. Whatever proves that reasonable creatures are *obliged* to love God and his law, proves that sinners are obliged to suitable hatred of sin, and abasement for it. A sinner cannot have due prevalent love to God, and hatred of sin, without prevalent *desire of obtaining deliverance from sin, and the enjoyment of God*. A suitable desire of ends so important cannot be without proportionable desire of the necessary means. If a sinner, therefore, who hears the Gospel, has these suitable affections, – of love to God, and hatred of sin, – to which he is obliged by the laws of natural religion, *these things cannot be separated from a real complacency in that redemption and grace which are proposed in revealed religion.* This does not suppose that natural religion can discover, or prove the peculiar things of the Gospel to be true; but, when they are discovered, it proves them to be infinitely desirable. A book of laws that are enforced with awful sanctions, cannot prove that the sovereign has passed an act of grace, or indemnity, in favour of transgressors; but it proves, that such favour is, to them, the most desirable and the most necessary thing in the world. It proves that the way of saving us from sin, which the Gospel reveals, is infinitely suitable to the honour of God, to the dignity of his law, and to the exigencies of the consciences of sinners." [2]

"If any man has a taste for moral excellence," says another, "a heart to account God glorious for being what he is, he cannot but see the moral excellency of the *law*, and love it, and conform to it, because it is the image of God; and so he cannot but see the moral excellency of the *Gospel*, and believe it, and love it, and comply with it; for it is also the image of God: he that can see the moral beauty in the original, cannot but see the moral beauty of the image drawn to life. He, therefore, that despises the Gospel, and is an enemy to the law, even he is at enmity against God himself. (*Romans 8:7*). Ignorance of the glory of God, and enmity against him, make men ignorant of the

---

2. M'Laurin's *Essay on Grace*, page 342.

glory of the law and of the Gospel, and enemies to both. Did men know and *love him that begat,* they would *love that which is begotten of him,* (*1 John 5:1*). *He that is of God heareth God's words: ye therefore hear them not, because ye are not of God,* (*John 8:47*)."[3]

III. THOUGH THE GOSPEL, STRICTLY SPEAKING, IS NOT A LAW, BUT A MESSAGE OF PURE GRACE, YET IT VIRTUALLY REQUIRES OBEDIENCE, AND SUCH AN OBEDIENCE AS INCLUDES SAVING FAITH.

It is no uncommon thing to distinguish between a formal requisition, and that which affords the *ground* or *reason* of that requisition. The *goodness* of God, for instance, though it is not a law or formal precept, yet virtually requires a return of gratitude. It deserves it; and the law of God formally requires it, on his behalf. Thus it is with respect to the Gospel, which is the greatest overflow of divine goodness that was ever displayed. A return suitable to its nature is required *virtually* by the Gospel itself; and *formally* by the divine precept, on its behalf.

I suppose it might be taken for granted, that the Gospel possesses some degree of virtual authority; as it is generally acknowledged, that, by reason of the dignity of its Author, and the importance of its subject matter, it deserves the *audience* and *attention* of all mankind; yea, more – that all mankind, who have opportunity of hearing it, are obliged to believe it. The only question, therefore, is, Whether the faith which it requires be spiritual, or such as has the promise of salvation?

We may form some idea of the manner in which the Gospel ought to be received, from its being represented as an embassy. *We are ambassadors for Christ,* saith the apostle, *as though God did beseech you by us: we pray you in Christ's stead, be ye* RECONCILED *to God.* (*2 Corinthians 5:20*). The object of an embassy, in all cases, is peace. Ambassadors are sometimes employed between friendly powers, for the adjustment of their affairs; but the allusion, in this case, is manifestly to a righteous prince, who should condescend to speak peaceably to his rebellious subjects, and, as it were, to entreat them, for their own sakes, to be reconciled. The language of the apostle supposes that the world is engaged in an unnatural and unprovoked rebellion

[margin note: unprovoked rebellion]

---

3. Bellamy's *True Religion Delineated*, page 332.

against its Maker; that it is in his power utterly to destroy sinners; that, if he were to deal with them according to their deserts, this must be their portion; but that, through the mediation of his Son, he had, as it were, suspended hostilities, had sent his servants with words of peace, and commissioned them to persuade, to entreat, and even to beseech them to be reconciled. But *reconciliation* to God includes everything that belongs to true conversion. It is the opposite of a state of *alienation and enmity* to him. (*Colossians 1:21*). It includes a justification of his government, a condemnation of their own unprovoked rebellion against him, and a thankful reception of the message of peace; which is the same, for substance, as to *repent and believe the Gospel.* To speak of an embassy from the God of heaven and earth to his rebellious creatures being entitled to nothing more than an *audience*, or a decent *attention*, must itself be highly offensive to the honour of his majesty; and that such language should proceed from his professed friends, must render it still more so.

"When the apostle beseecheth us to be *reconciled* to God, I would know," says Dr Owen, "whether it be not a part of our duty to yield obedience? If not, the exhortation is frivolous and vain."[4] If sinners are not obliged to be reconciled to God, both as a Lawgiver and a Saviour, and that with all their hearts, it is no sin to be unreconciled. All the enmity of their hearts to God, his law, his Gospel, or his Son, must be guiltless. For there can be no neutrality in this case: not to be reconciled, is to be unreconciled; not to fall in with the message of peace, is to fall out with it; and not to lay down arms, and submit to mercy, is to maintain the war.

It is in perfect harmony with the foregoing ideas, that those who acquiesce in the way of salvation in this spiritual manner, are represented, in so doing, as exercising OBEDIENCE; as *obeying the Gospel, obeying the truth*, and *obeying Christ*. (*Romans 10:16; 6:17*). The very end of the Gospel being preached is said to be, for obedience to the faith among all nations, (*Romans 1:5*). But *obedience* supposes previous obligation. If repentance towards God, and faith towards our Lord Jesus Christ, were not duties required of us, even prior to all consideration of their being blessings bestowed upon us, it were incongruous to speak of them as exercises of *obedience*. Nor would it be less so, to speak of that impenitence and unbelief, which

4. *Display of Arminianism*, chapter 10.

expose men to *eternal destruction from the presence of the Lord, and from the glory of his power*, as consisting in their not obeying the Gospel. (*2 Thessalonians 1:8, 9*). The passage on which the former part of this argument is founded, (*2 Corinthians 5:19, 20*), has been thought inapplicable to the subject, because it is supposed to be *an address to the members of the church at Corinth*, who were considered by the apostle as believers. But let it be considered, whether the apostle be here immediately addressing the members of the church at Corinth, beseeching them, at that time, to be reconciled to God; or, whether he be not rather *rehearsing to them what had been his conduct, and that of his brethren in the ministry, in vindication of himself and them from the base insinuations of false teachers;* to whom the great evils that had crept into that church had been principally owing? The methods they appear to have taken to supplant the apostles, were those of underhand insinuation. By Paul's answers, they appear to have suggested that he and his friends were either subtle men, who, by their *soft* and *beseeching* style, ingratiated themselves into the esteem of the simple, catching them, as it were, *with guile,* (*2 Corinthians 1:12; 12:16*), or weak-headed enthusiasts, *beside themselves,* (*2 Corinthians 5:13*), going up and down, *beseeching* people to this and that, (*2 Corinthians 11:21*); and that, as to Paul himself, however great he might appear in his *letters*, he was nothing in company. *His bodily presence,* say they, *is weak, and his speech contemptible,* (*2 Corinthians 10:10*).

In the first epistle to this church, Paul generously waived a defence of himself and his brethren, being more concerned for the recovery of those to Christ who were in danger of being drawn off from the truth as it is in Jesus, than respecting their opinion of him. Yet, when the one was accomplished, he undertook the other; not only as a justification of himself and his brethren, but as knowing that just sentiments of faithful ministers bore an intimate connection with the spiritual welfare of their hearers. It is thus that the apostle alludes to their various insinuations, acknowledging that they did indeed *beseech, entreat,* and *persuade* men, but affirming that such conduct arose not from the motives of which they were accused, but from the *love of Christ. If we are beside ourselves, it is for your sakes.*

If the words in *2 Corinthians 5:19, 20* be an immediate address to the *members* of the church at Corinth, those which follow, in

2 Corinthians 6:1 must be an address to its ministers. But, if so, the apostle, in the continuation of that address, would not have said as he does, *In all things approving* OURSELVES *as the ministers of God.* His language would have been, In all things approving YOURSELVES, etc. Hence it is manifest that the whole is a vindication of their preaching and manner of life, against the insinuations of the Corinthian teachers.

There are two things which may have contributed to the mis-understanding of this passage of Scripture. One is, the supplement *you,* which is unnecessarily introduced three times over in *2 Corinthians 5:20,* and *6:1.* If any supplement had been necessary, the word *men,* as it is in the text of *2 Corinthians 5:11,* might have better conveyed the apostle's meaning. The other is, the division of *2 Corinthians 5* and *6* in the midst of the argument.

IV. THE WANT OF FAITH IN CHRIST IS ASCRIBED, IN THE SCRIPTURES, TO MEN'S DEPRAVITY, AND IS ITSELF REPRESENTED AS A HEINOUS SIN.

It is taken for granted, that whatever is not a sinner's duty, the omission of it cannot be charged on him as a sin, nor imputed to any depravity in him. If faith were no more a duty than *election* or *redemption,* which are acts peculiar to God, the want of the one would be no more ascribed to the evil dispositions of the heart, than of the other. Or, if the inability of sinners to believe in Christ were of the same nature as that of a dead body in a grave to rise up and walk, it were absurd to suppose that they would, on this account, fall under the divine censure. No man is reproved for not doing that which is naturally impossible; but sinners *are* reproved for not believing, and given to understand that it is solely owing to their criminal ignorance, pride, dishonesty of heart, and aversion from God.

Voluntary ignorance is represented as a reason why sinners believe not. *Being* IGNORANT *of God's righteousness, and going about to establish their own righteousness,* THEY HAVE NOT SUBMITTED THEMSELVES UNTO THE RIGHTEOUSNESS OF GOD. – *If our Gospel be hid, it is hid to them that are lost: in whom the God of this world hath* BLINDED THE MINDS OF THEM WHICH BELIEVE NOT, *lest the light of the glorious Gospel of Christ, who is the image of God, should shine* unto them. (*Romans 10:3; 2 Corinthians 4:3, 4*). To the same purpose, we are taught by our Lord, in the parable of the sower: *When any one heareth the word of the kingdom, and* UNDERSTANDETH IT NOT, *then cometh the wicked one, and catcheth away that which was sown in his heart;* and this, as Luke expresses it, *lest they should* BELIEVE AND BE SAVED. (*Matthew 13:19; Luke 8:12*).

If men, even though they were possessed of the same principles as our first father in paradise, would nevertheless be blind to the glory of the Gospel, with what propriety is their blindness attributed to the god of this world? Is he ever represented as employing himself in hindering that which is naturally impossible, or in promoting that which is innocent?

Pride is another cause to which the want of saving faith is ascribed. *The wicked, through the pride of his countenance, will not seek after God: God is not in all his thoughts.* (*Psalm 10:4*). We have seen already that *seeking* God is a spiritual exercise, which implies faith in the Mediator; and the reason why ungodly men are strangers to it is, the haughtiness of their spirits, which makes them scorn to take the place of supplicants before their offended Creator, and labour to put far from their minds every thought of him. *How can ye* BELIEVE, said our Lord to the Jews, *which receive honour one of another, and seek not the honour that cometh from God only?* (*John 5:44*).

If believing were here to be taken for any other faith than that which is spiritual or saving, the suggestion would not hold good; for we are told of some who *could* and *did* believe in Christ, in some sense, but who did not confess him, for they *loved the praise of men more than the praise of God.* (*John 12:43*). It was *pride* that blinded the minds of the *wise and prudent of this world* to the doctrines of Christ; and what is it but this same proud spirit, working in a way of self-conceit and self-righteousness, that still forms the grand objection to the doctrine of salvation by mere grace?

Dishonesty of heart is that on account of which men receive not the word of God, so as to bring forth fruit. This is fully implied in the parable of the sower, recorded in *Luke 8*. The reason why those hearers represented by the good ground received the word, and brought forth good fruit, rather than the others, was that they had *good and honest hearts* – plainly intimating that the reason why the others did not so receive it, was that their hearts were not *upright honest heart explained*

before God. Indeed, such is the nature of divine truth, that every heart which is honest towards God must receive it. An honest heart must needs approve of God's holy law, which requires us to love him with all our powers; and this, because it is no more than giving him the glory due to his name. An honest heart will approve of being justified wholly for Christ's sake, and not on account of any of its own works, whether legal or evangelical; for it is no more than relinquishing a claim which is justly forfeited, and accepting, as a free gift, that which God was under no obligation to bestow. Further: an honest heart must rejoice in the way of salvation, as soon as he understands it; because it provides a way in which mercy can be exercised *consistently with righteousness.* A right spirit would revolt at the idea of receiving mercy itself in a way that should leave a blot upon the divine character. It is the glory of Christ that he has not an honest man for an enemy. *The upright love him.*

We are not ignorant who it is that must now give men honest hearts, and what is the source of everything, in a fallen creature, that is truly good; but this does not affect the argument. However far sinners are from it, and whatever divine agency it may require to produce it, no man who is not disposed to deny the accountability of creatures to the God that made them will deny that, to be honest in heart is their duty; for if we are not obliged to be upright towards God, we are obliged to nothing; and if obliged to nothing, we must be guiltless, and so stand in no need of salvation.

Further: *aversion of heart* is assigned as a reason why sinners do not believe. This truth is strongly expressed in that complaint of our Lord in *John 5:40: Ye will not,* or YE ARE NOT WILLING, *to come to me, that ye might have life.* Proudly attached to their own righteousness, when Jesus exhibited himself as *the way, the truth, and the life,* they were stumbled at it; and thousands, in the religious world, are the same to this day. They are willing to escape God's wrath, and to gain his favour – yea, and to relinquish many an outward vice in order to it; but *to come to Jesus* among the chief of sinners, and be indebted wholly to his sacrifice for life, they are *not willing.* Yet, can any man plead that this their unwillingness is innocent?

There is no inconsistency between this account of things, and that which is given elsewhere, that *no man* CAN *come to Christ, except the*

Father draw him, (*John 6:44*). No man *can* choose that from which his heart is averse. It is common, both in Scripture and in conversation, to speak of a person who is under the influence of an evil bias of heart, as unable to do that which is inconsistent with it. *They have eyes full of adultery, and* CANNOT *cease from sin. – The carnal mind is enmity against God: for it is not subject to the law of God, neither indeed* CAN *be. So then they that are in the flesh* CANNOT *please God.* (*2 Peter 2:14; Romans 8:7, 8*).

On account of this different phraseology, some writers have affirmed that men are under both a moral and a natural inability of coming to Christ; or that they *neither will nor can* come to him. But, if there be no other inability than what arises from aversion, this language is not accurate; for it conveys the idea, that, if all aversion of heart were removed, there would still be a natural and insurmountable bar in the way. But no such idea as this is conveyed by our Lord's words. The only bar to which he refers, lies in that *reluctance* or *aversion* which the drawing of the Father implies and removes. Nor will such an idea comport with what he elsewhere teaches. *And because I tell you the truth, ye believe me not. Which of you convinceth me of sin? And if I say the truth, why do ye not believe me? He that is of God heareth God's words: ye therefore hear them not, because ye are not of God. – Why do ye not understand my speech?* BECAUSE YE CANNOT HEAR MY WORD. (*John 8:43, 45-47*). These cutting interrogations proceed on the supposition that they *could have received the doctrine of Christ, if it had been agreeable to their corrupt hearts; and its being otherwise was the* ONLY *reason why they could not understand and believe it.* If sinners were naturally and absolutely unable to believe in Christ, they would be equally unable to disbelieve; for it requires the same powers to reject, as to embrace. And in this case there would be no room for an inability of another kind. A dead body is equally unable to do evil as to do good; and a man naturally and absolutely blind could not be guilty of shutting his eyes against the light. "It is indwelling sin," as Dr Owen says, "that both disenableth men unto, and hinders them from believing, AND THAT ALONE. Blindness of mind, stubbornness of the will, sensuality of the affections, all concur to keep poor perishing souls at a distance from Christ. Men are made blind by sin, and cannot see his excellency; obstinate, and will not lay hold of his righteousness; senseless, and take no notice of their eternal concernments." [5]

A voluntary and judicial blindness, obstinacy, and hardness of heart, are represented as the bar to conversion. (*Acts 28:27*). But if that spirit which is exercised in conversion were essentially different from anything which the subjects of it, in any state, possessed, or ought to have possessed, it were absurd to ascribe the want of it to such causes.

Those who embraced the Gospel, and submitted to the government of the Messiah, were baptised with the baptism of John, and are said, in so doing, to have *justified* God. Their conduct was an acknowledgment of the justice of the law, and of the wisdom and love of the Gospel. On the other hand, those who did not thus submit, are said to have *rejected the counsel of God against themselves.* (*Luke 7:30*). How, then, can this passage be understood, but by supposing that they *ought* to have repented of their sins, embraced the Messiah, and submitted to his ordinances?

Finally. *Unbelief is expressly declared to be a sin, of which the Spirit of truth has to convince the world, (John 16:8, 9).* But unbelief cannot be a sin, if faith were not a duty. I know of no answer to this argument, but what must be drawn from a distinction between believing the report of the Gospel, and saving faith; allowing the want of the one to be sinful, but not of the other. But it is not of gross unbelief only, or of an open rejection of Jesus as the Messiah, that the Holy Spirit has to convince the world; nor is it to a bare conviction of this truth, like what prevails in all Christian countries, that men are brought by his teaching. When he, the Spirit of truth, cometh, his operations are *deeper* than this amounts to. It is of an *opposition of heart* to the way of salvation that he convinces the sinner, and to a cordial acquiescence with it that he brings him. Those who are born in a Christian land, and who never were the subjects of gross infidelity, stand in no less need of being thus convinced than others. Nay, in some respects they need it more. Their unbelieving opposition to Christ is more subtle, refined, and out of sight, than that of open infidels. They are less apt, therefore, to suspect themselves of it, and, consequently, stand in greater need of the Holy Spirit to search them out, and show them to themselves. Amongst those who

5. *On Indwelling Sin*, chapter 16.

constantly sit under the Gospel, and who remain in an unconverted state, there are few who think themselves the enemies of Christ. On the contrary, they flatter themselves that they are willing, at any time, to be converted, if God would but convert them; considering themselves as lying at the pool for the moving of the waters. But *when he, the Spirit of truth, cometh,* these coverings will be stripped from off the face, and these refuges of lies will fail. [6]

V. GOD HAS THREATENED AND INFLICTED THE MOST AWFUL PUNISHMENTS ON SINNERS FOR THEIR NOT BELIEVING ON THE LORD JESUS CHRIST.

It is here taken for granted, that nothing but sin can be the cause of God's inflicting punishment; and nothing can be sin, which is not a breach of duty.

Go ye into all the world, and preach the Gospel to every creature. He that believeth and is baptised shall be saved; BUT HE THAT BELIEVETH NOT SHALL BE DAMNED. (*Mark 16:15, 16*). This awful passage appears to be a kind of *ultimatum,* or last resolve. It is as if our Lord had said, "This is your message ... go and proclaim it to all nations: whosoever receives it, and submits to my authority, assure him, from me, that eternal salvation awaits him; but whosoever rejects it, let him see to it ... damnation shall be his portion!" *Believing* and *not believing,* in this passage, serve to explain each other. It is saving faith, to which salvation is promised; and to the want of this it is, that damnation is threatened.

It has been alleged that, "as it is not inferable, from that declaration, that the faith of believers is the procuring cause of their salvation, so it is not to be inferred, from thence, that the want of that *special* faith in unbelievers is the procuring cause of their damnation. That declaration contains in it the descriptive characters of those who are saved, and of those who are damned; but it assigns not special faith to be the procuring cause of the salvation of the former, nor the want of it to be the procuring cause of the damnation of the latter." [7]

But if this mode of reasoning were admitted, we should find it very difficult, if not impossible, to prove anything to be evil, from

---

6. See Charnock's excellent discourse, on *Unbelief the Greatest Sin,* in volume 2 of his *Works.*

7. Mr Brine's *Motives to Love and Unity,* pages 31, 32.

the threatenings of God against it. A multitude of plain texts of Scripture, wherein sin, as any common reader would suppose, is threatened with punishment, might, in this manner, be made to teach nothing with regard to its being the procuring cause of it. For example, *Psalm 37:18. 20: The Lord knoweth the days of the upright: and their inheritance shall be for ever ... But the wicked shall perish, and the enemies of the Lord shall be as the fat of lambs: they shall consume; into smoke shall they consume away.* But it might be said, as the uprightness of the upright is not the procuring cause of his enjoying an everlasting inheritance, so neither will this prove that the wickedness of the wicked, or the enmity of the Lord's enemies, is the procuring cause of their being consumed. Again, *Psalm 147:6: The Lord lifteth up the meek: he casteth the wicked down to the ground.* But it might be alleged that, as the meekness of the former is not the procuring cause of his being lifted up, so it cannot be, from hence, inferred, that the wickedness of the latter is the procuring cause of his being cast down. Again, *Psalm 145:20: The Lord preserveth all them that love him: but all the wicked will he destroy.* But it might be said, as the love of the one is not the procuring cause of his preservation, so it cannot be proved from hence, that the wickedness of the other is the procuring cause of his destruction; and that these declarations contain only the *descriptive characters* of those who are saved, and of those who perish.

In this manner, almost all the threatenings in the book of God might be made to say nothing as *threatenings;* for the mode in which they are delivered is the same as that in the passage in question. For example, *What shall be given unto thee? or what shall be done unto thee, thou false tongue? Sharp arrows of the mighty, with coals of juniper. – He that showeth no mercy, shall have judgment without mercy. – Whoremongers and adulterers God will judge. – Be not deceived: neither fornicators, nor idolaters, nor adulterers, nor effeminate, nor abusers of themselves with mankind, nor thieves, nor covetous, nor drunkards, nor revilers, nor extortioners, shall inherit the kingdom of God. – Behold, the day cometh, that shall burn as an oven; and all the proud, yea, and all that do wickedly, shall be stubble. – Bring hither those mine enemies, which would not that I should reign over them, and slay them before me. – The fearful, and unbelieving, and the abominable, and murderers, and whoremongers, and sorcerers, and idolaters, and all liars, shall have their part in the lake which burneth with fire and brimstone: which is the second death.* (*Psalm 120:3, 4; James 2:13; Hebrews 13:4; 1 Corinthians 6:9, 10; Malachi 4:1; Luke 19:27; Revelation 21:8*). But none of these awful threatenings declare that the respective crimes, which are mentioned, are the procuring cause of the evils denounced. Though it is said, concerning the *false tongue*, that *sharp arrows of the mighty, with coals of juniper, shall be given him*, yet it does not say that these shall be given him *because* of his falsehood; and so on, of the rest. And thus they may be only descriptive characters of those who shall be damned; and all these things may, for all these denunciations prove, be blameless. If this reasoning be just, it cannot be inferred, from the laws of England declaring that a murderer shall be put to death, that it is *on account* of his being a murderer. Neither could our first parents justly infer, from its being told them, *The day ye eat thereof ye shall surely die*, that it should be *on that account.*

The truth is, though eternal life be the *gift of God*, yet eternal death is the proper WAGES of sin: and though faith is not represented, in the above passage, as the procuring cause of salvation, yet unbelief is of damnation. It is common for the Scriptures to describe those that shall be saved, by something which is pleasing to God, and by which they are made meet for glory; and those that shall be lost, by something which is displeasing to God, and by which they are fitted for destruction.

John 3:18. – He that believeth on him is not condemned: but he that believeth not is condemned already, BECAUSE *he hath not believed in the name of the only begotten Son of God.*

Two things are here observable. *First: Believing* is expressive of saving faith, seeing it exempts from *condemnation. Second:* The want of this faith is a sin, on account of which the unbeliever stands condemned. It is true, that unbelief is an *evidence* of our being under the condemnation of God's righteous law for all our *other sins;* but this is not all; unbelief is *itself* a sin, which greatly aggravates our guilt, and which, if persisted in, gives the finishing stroke to our destruction. That this idea is taught by the evangelist appears, partly from his dwelling upon the dignity of the character offended, *the only begotten Son of God;* and partly from his expressly adding, *This is* THE CONDEMNATION, *that light is come into the world, and men loved darkness rather than light, because their deeds were evil. (verse 19).*

> *Luke 19:27. — But those mine enemies, which would not that I should reign over them, bring hither, and slay them before me.*

If Christ, as wearing his mediatorial crown, has not a right to unreserved submission and hearty obedience, he has no right to be angry; and still less to punish men as his enemies, for not being willing that he should reign over them. He has no right to reign over them, at least not over their hearts, if it be not their duty to obey him from their hearts. The whole controversy, indeed, might be reduced to an issue on this argument. Every sinner ought to be Christ's friend, or his enemy, or to stand by as neutral. To say he ought to be his enemy, is too gross to be defended. To plead for his being neutral, is pleading for what our Lord declares to be impossible: *he that is not with me is against me.* There is, therefore, no room for any other position, than that he ought to be his cordial friend; and this is the plain implication of the passage.

> *2 Thessalonians 2:9-12. — Whose coming is … with all deceivableness of unrighteousness in them that perish; because they received not the love of the truth, that they might be saved. And for this cause God shall send them strong delusion, that they should believe a lie: that they all might be damned who believed not the truth, but had pleasure in unrighteousness.*

From hence, we may remark two things. *First:* That faith is here called a *receiving the love of the truth;* and that it means saving faith, is manifest, seeing it is added, *that they might be saved. Secondly:* That their not receiving the love of the truth, or, which is the same thing, not believing with such a faith as that to which salvation is promised, was the *cause* of their being given up of God, and carried away with all deceivableness of unrighteousness. The loose and cold-hearted manner in which merely nominal Christians held the truth, would occasion the introduction of the grand papal apostasy, by which great numbers of them would be swept away. And this, assuredly, ought to afford a lesson to nominal Christians of the present day, who, owing to the same cause, are fast approaching to infidelity. But, unless we suppose that these professors of religion ought to have *received the love of the truth*, there is no accounting for the awful judgments of God upon them for the contrary.

VI. OTHER SPIRITUAL EXERCISES, WHICH SUSTAIN AN INSEPARABLE CONNECTION WITH FAITH IN CHRIST, ARE REPRESENTED AS THE DUTY OF MEN IN GENERAL.

Though this controversy has been mostly carried on with respect to the duty of *faith*, yet it, in reality, extends to the whole of spiritual religion. Those who deny that sinners are obliged to believe in Christ for salvation, will not allow that it is their duty to do anything truly and spiritually good. It is a kind of maxim with such persons, that "none can be obliged to act spiritually, but spiritual men." *Spiritual* exercises appear to me to mean the same as *holy* exercises; for the *new man, which is created after God*, is said to be *created in righteousness, and* TRUE HOLINESS; and as to two kinds of true holiness, the Scriptures, I believe, are silent. But as some writers affix different ideas to the term *spiritual;* to prevent all disputes about it, I shall proceed on a ground which they will not refuse.

Whatever has the promise of spiritual blessings, is considered as a spiritual exercise. With this criterion of spirituality in view, let the following passages of Scripture be carefully considered:

How long, ye simple ones, will ye love simplicity? and the scorners delight in their scorning, and fools hate knowledge? Turn you at my reproof: behold, I will pour out my Spirit unto you, I will make known my words unto you. — The fear of the Lord is the beginning of knowledge: but fools despise wisdom and instruction. — Wisdom crieth at the gates, at the entry of the city, at the coming in at the doors. Unto you, O men, I call; and my voice is to the sons of man. O ye simple, understand wisdom: and, ye fools, be ye of an understanding heart. Hear; for I will speak of excellent things; and the opening of my lips shall be right things. — Receive my instruction, and not silver; and knowledge rather than choice gold. — Hearken unto me, O ye children: for blessed are they that keep my ways. Hear instruction, and be wise, and refuse it not. Blessed is the man that heareth me, watching daily at my gates, waiting at the posts of my doors. For whoso findeth me findeth life, and shall obtain favour of the Lord. But he that sinneth against me wrongeth his own soul: all they that hate me love death. — And *now, Israel, what doth the Lord thy God require of thee, but to* FEAR *the Lord thy God, to walk in* ALL *his ways, and to* LOVE *him, and to* SERVE *the Lord thy God with* ALL THY HEART AND WITH ALL THY SOUL? – Circumcise therefore the foreskin of your heart, and be no more stiff-necked. – Rend your* HEART, *and not your garments, and turn unto the Lord your God. – Repent ye: for the kingdom of heaven is at hand. –* REPENT *ye therefore, and be* CONVERTED, *that your sins may be blotted out, when the times of refreshing shall come from the presence of the Lord. (Proverbs 1:22, 23, 7; 8:3-6, 10, 32-36; Deuteronomy 10:12, 16; Joel 2:13; Matthew 3:2; Acts 3:19).*

We may remark on these passages, *First:* The persons addressed were *unconverted sinners,* as appears by their characters; *fools – scorners – haters of knowledge – uncircumcised in heart – impenitent. Second:* The things to which they were exhorted were things *spiritually good.* This appears, in part, from the names by which the exercises themselves are denominated; namely, such understanding as originates in *the fear of the Lord – fearing – loving – serving God with all the heart, and with all the soul – circumcision of the heart – repentance – conversion;* and, partly, from the blessings of salvation being promised to them: these are expressed by the terms *blessedness – life – favour of the Lord – the blotting out of sin.*

More particularly: *The love of God* is a spiritual exercise; for it has the promise of spiritual blessings. *All things work together for good to them that love God. – He that dwelleth in love dwelleth in God, and God in him. – Eye hath not seen, nor ear heard, neither have entered into the heart of man, the things which God hath prepared for them that love him. (Romans 8:28; 1 John 4:16; 1 Corinthians 2:9).* But the love of God is required of men without distinction. The people of Israel, like all other people, were composed of good and bad men; but they were all required to *love* Jehovah, and to *cleave* to him, and that with *all their heart, and soul, and mind, and strength. (Deuteronomy 6:5; 30:20).* The moral part of those precepts which God gave to them on tables of stone, were binding on all mankind. Even those who had no other means of knowing God than were afforded by the works of nature, with, perhaps, a portion of tradition, were required to GLORIFY HIM AS GOD, AND TO BE THANKFUL. (*Romans 1:21*).

The love of God, as is here intimated, is either a holy *thankfulness* for the innumerable instances of his goodness, or a cordial approbation of his *glorious character*. It is true, there are favours for which the regenerate are obliged to love Him, which are not common to the unregenerate: but everyone has shared a sufficient portion of his bounty to have incurred a debt of gratitude. It is generally allowed, indeed, that God ought to be loved as our Creator and Benefactor; but this, they suppose, is not a spiritual exercise. There is a kind of gratitude, it is granted, which is not spiritual, but merely the effect of natural self-love, and in which God is no otherwise regarded than as subservient to our happiness. But this does not always respect the bestowing of temporal mercies: the same feelings which possessed the carnal Israelites, when they felt themselves delivered from Pharaoh's yoke, and saw their oppressors sinking in the sea, are still the feelings of many professors of religion, under a groundless persuasion of their being elected of God, and having their sins forgiven them. Gratitude of this sort has nothing spiritual in it: but then, neither is it any part of duty. God nowhere requires it, either of saints or sinners. That which God requires is a *spiritual* exercise: whether it be on account of temporal or spiritual mercies, is immaterial; the object makes no difference as to the nature of the act: that *thanksgiving* with which the common mercies of life are received by the godly, and by which they are *sanctified* to them, (*1 Timothy 4:3, 4*), is no less of a spiritual nature, and is no less connected with eternal life, than gratitude for the forgiveness of sin. This thankful spirit, instead of being an operation of self-love, or regarding God merely in subserviency to our own happiness, greatly consists in self-abasement, or in a sense of our own unworthiness. Its language is, *Who am I, O Lord God? and what is my house, that thou hast brought me hitherto? – What shall I render unto the Lord for all his benefits?* This is *holy* gratitude; and to be destitute of it, is to be *unthankful, unholy*.

With respect to a *cordial approbation of the divine character, or glorifying God as God*, and which enters into the essence of holy love, there can be no reasonable doubt whether it be obligatory on sinners. Such is the glory of God's *name*, that nothing but the most inexcusable and deep-rooted depravity could render any intelligent creature unconscious of it. Those parts of Scripture which describe the devout feelings of godly men, particularly the *Psalms of David*, abound in expressions of affection to the NAME of the Lord.

> *How excellent is thy* NAME *in all the earth! – Not unto us, O Lord, not unto us, but unto thy* NAME *give glory. – O magnify the Lord with me, and let us exalt his* NAME *together. – Sing unto God, sing praises to his* NAME: *let them that love thy* NAME *say continually, The Lord be magnified. – Blessed be his glorious* NAME *for ever: and let the whole earth be filled with his glory; Amen, and Amen.* (*Psalm 8:1; 115:1; 34:3; 40:16; 72:19*).

This affection to the *name* of the Lord, as it is revealed in his Word and works, and particularly in the work of redemption, lies at the foundation of all true desire after an interest in his mercy. If we seek mercy of anyone whose character we disesteem, it is merely for our own sakes; and if he be acquainted with our motives, we cannot hope to succeed. This it is that leads us to mourn for sin as sin, and not merely for the inconvenience to which it exposes us. This it is which renders salvation through the atonement of Christ so acceptable. He that loves only himself, provided he might be saved, would care little or nothing for the honour of the divine character: but he that loves God, will be concerned for his glory. Heaven itself would be no enjoyment to him, if his admission must be at the expense of righteousness.

"God is to be loved," says Dr Gill, "for himself; because of his own nature, and the perfections of it, which render him amiable and lovely, and worthy of our strongest love and affection; as these are displayed in the works of creation and providence, and especially of grace, redemption, and salvation; to all which the Psalmist has respect, when he says, *O Lord our Lord, how excellent is thy* NAME, – nature, and perfections, – *in all the earth! (Psalm 8:1).* As God is great in himself, and greatly to be praised; great, and greatly to be feared; so he is great, and greatly to be loved, for what he is in himself. And this is the purest and most perfect love of a creature towards God; for, if we love him only for his goodness towards us, it is loving ourselves rather than him, at least, a loving him for ourselves, and so a loving ourselves more than him." But this "most pure and perfect love" is manifestly the duty of all mankind, however far they are from a compliance with it. *Give unto the Lord, ye kindreds of the people, give unto the Lord glory and strength. Give unto the Lord the glory* DUE *unto his name: bring an offering, and come before him: worship the Lord in the beauty of holiness. – Make a joyful noise unto the Lord, all ye lands. – Kings of the earth, and all people; princes, and all judges of the earth: both young men, and maidens; old men, and children: let them praise the name of the Lord:* FOR HIS NAME ALONE IS EXCELLENT; *his glory is above the earth and heaven. – Let the people praise thee, O God; let all the people praise thee!* (*1 Chronicles 16:28, 29; Psalm 100:1; 148:11-13; 67:3*).

That *love to Christ* is a spiritual exercise, may, I suppose, be taken for granted. The *grace*, or favour of God, is with all who possess it *in sincerity.* (*Ephesians 6:24*). But love to Christ is the duty of everyone to whom the Gospel is preached. On no other principles could the apostle have written as he did: *If any man love not the Lord Jesus Christ, let him be Anathema Maran-atha!* It is worthy of notice, that this awful sentence is not denounced against sinners, as positively hating Christ, but as not loving him; plainly implying his *worthiness* of a place in our best affections, and that, were it possible for us to be indifferent towards him, even that indifference would deserve the heavy curse of the Almighty at the last judgment. Paul appears to have felt as a soldier would feel towards the best of princes, or commanders. If, after David's return from his engagement with Goliath, when the women of Israel were praising him in their songs, any of the sons of Belial had spoken of him in the language of detraction, it would have been natural, for one of a patriotic spirit, deeply impressed with an idea of the hero's worth, and of the service he had rendered to his country, thus to have expressed himself: "If any man love not the son of Jesse, let him be banished from among the tribes of Israel." Of this kind were the feelings of the apostle. He had served under his Lord and Saviour for many years: and now, conscious in a high degree of the glory of his character, he scruples not to pronounce that man who loves him not, *accursed!*

The fear of God is a spiritual exercise; for it has the promise of spiritual blessings. (*Psalm 34:7, 9; 103:11, 13, 17*). But it is also a duty required of men, and that without the distinction of being regenerate or unregenerate. *O that there were such an heart in them, that they would* FEAR *me, and keep all my commandments always!*

– FEAR *before him, all the earth.* – *Let all that be round about him bring presents unto him* THAT OUGHT TO BE FEARED. – *Who would not* FEAR *thee, O King of nations?* – FEAR *thou God.* – FEAR *God, and keep his commandments: for this is the whole duty of man.* – *Gather the people together, men, and women, and children, and thy stranger that is within thy gates, that they may hear, and that they may learn, and* FEAR *the Lord your God ... and that their children, which have not known any thing, may hear, and learn to* FEAR *the Lord your God.* – *Serve the Lord with* FEAR, *and rejoice with trembling.* – *And I saw another angel fly in the midst of heaven, having the everlasting Gospel to preach unto them that dwell on the earth, and to every nation, and kindred, and tongue, and people, saying, ...* FEAR GOD, *and give glory to him; for the hour of his judgment is come: and worship him that made heaven, and earth!* – *Who shall not* FEAR *thee, O Lord, and glorify thy name? for thou only art holy,* (*Deuteronomy 5:29; 1 Chronicles 16:30; Psalm 76:11; Jeremiah 10:7; Ecclesiastes 5:7, 12:13; Deuteronomy 31:12, 13; Psalm 2:11; Revelation 14:6, 7; 15:4*). To say of men, *they have no fear of God before their eyes,* (*Romans 3:18*), is to represent them as under the dominion of depravity.

It may be objected, that the Scriptures distinguish between that holy fear of offending God which is peculiar to his children, and a mere dread of the misery threatened against sin, which is found in the wicked. True; there is a fear of God which is not spiritual: such was that of the slothful servant; and the same is found in hypocrites and devils, (*Luke 19:21; James 2:19*): this, however, is no part of duty, but rather of punishment. God does not require this, either of saints or sinners. That which he requires, is of a *holy* nature, such as is expressed in the passages before quoted; which is spiritual, and has the promise of spiritual blessings. It resembles that of a dutiful child to his father, and is therefore properly called *filial;* and though none are possessed of it but the children of God, yet that is because none else are possessed of a right spirit.

Repentance, or a *godly sorrow for sin,* is a spiritual exercise; for it abounds with promises of spiritual blessings. But repentance is a duty required of every sinner. *Repent ye: for the kingdom of heaven is at hand.* – *Repent ye therefore, and be converted, that your sins may be blotted out.* – *Cleanse your hands, ye sinners; and purify your hearts, ye double minded. Be afflicted, and mourn, and weep: let your laughter be turned to mourning, and your joy to heaviness. Humble yourselves in the sight of the Lord, and he shall lift you up.* (*Matthew 3:2; Acts 3:19; James 4:8-10*). The *hardness of heart* which our Lord found in the Jews, and which is the opposite of repentance, *grieved* him: which it would not, had it not been their sin, (*Mark 3:5*). Finally: *A hard and impenitent heart treasures up wrath against the day of wrath:* but impenitence could be no sin, if penitence were not a duty. (*Romans 2:5*).

Repentance, it is allowed, like all other spiritual exercises, has its counterfeit, and which is not spiritual; but neither is it that which God requires at the hands of either saints or sinners. What is called natural, and sometimes legal repentance, is merely a sorrow on account of *consequences*. Such was the repentance of Saul and Judas.

In order to evade the argument arising from the addresses of John the Baptist, of Christ and his apostles, who called upon the Jewish people *to repent, and believe the Gospel*, it has been alleged that it was only an outward repentance and acknowledgment of the truth to which they were exhorted, and not that which is spiritual, or which has the promise of spiritual blessings. But it will be difficult, if not impossible, to prove that such repentance and faith are anywhere required of sinners, or that it is consistent with the divine perfections to require them. An outward repentance and reformation of manners, as distinguished from that which consists in godly sorrow, is only *repentance in appearance*. Whatever sorrow there is in it, it is not on account of sin, but its consequences; and to suppose that Christ, or his servants, required this, would be doing them an infinite dishonour. It is no other than supposing them to have betrayed the authority of God over the human heart; to have sanctioned hypocrisy; and to have given counsels to sinners, which, if taken, would leave them still exposed to everlasting destruction.

The case of the Ninevites has been alleged as furnishing an example of that repentance which is the duty of men in general, and which Christ and his apostles required of the Jews. I do not know that the repentance of the Ninevites was genuine, or connected with spiritual blessings; neither does anyone know that it was not. Probably, the repentance of some of them was genuine, while that of the greater part might be only put on in conformity to the orders of government; or, at most, merely as the effect of terror. But, whatever it was, even if none of it was genuine, the object *professed* was *godly sorrow for sin;* and if God treated them upon the supposition of their being sincere, and it repented him of the evil which he had threatened, it is no more than he did to Pharaoh, Abijah, Ahab, and others. (*Exodus 8:8, 9; 2 Chronicles 13* with *1 Kings 15; 1 Kings 21:27-29*). It is a very unjust conclusion to draw from his conduct, that their repentance was such as he approved, and the whole which he required at their hands. So far from it, there might be nothing in any of them which could approve itself to him as the Searcher of hearts; and though, for wise reasons, he might think it proper, in those instances, to overlook their hypocrisy, and to *treat* them on the supposition of their repentance being what they professed it to be, yet he might still reserve to himself the power of judging them at the last day according to their works.

The object of John the Baptist was not to effect a mere outward reformation of manners, but to *turn the hearts of the fathers to the children, and the disobedient to the wisdom of the just; to make ready a people prepared for the Lord.* (*Luke 1:17*). Such was the effect actually produced by his ministry, and by that of Christ and the apostles. The repentance which they called upon sinners to exercise, was such as had the promise of *the remission of sins*, (*Mark 1:4; Acts 2:38*).

It is plainly intimated, by the apostle Paul, that all repentance, except that which works in a way of godly sorrow, and which he calls *repentance to salvation*, NEEDS TO BE REPENTED OF. It is the mere *sorrow of the world*, which *worketh death*, (*2 Corinthians 7:10*). But that which requires to be repented of, cannot be commanded of God, or constitute any part of a sinner's duty. The duty of every transgressor is to be *sorry at heart* for having sinned.

Humility, or *lowliness of mind*, is a spiritual disposition, and has the promise of spiritual blessings. *Though the Lord be high, yet hath he respect unto the lowly. – He giveth grace unto the humble. – Blessed are the poor in spirit: for theirs is the kingdom of heaven,* (*Psalm 138:6; James 4:6; Matthew 5:3*): yet this disposition is required as the duty of all. *Cleanse your hands, ye sinners; and purify your hearts, ye double minded. Be afflicted, and mourn, and weep: let your laughter be turned to mourning, and your joy to heaviness. Humble yourselves in the sight of the Lord, and he shall lift you up,* (*James 4:8-10*). Humility does not consist in thinking less or more meanly of ourselves than is true. The difference between one that is lowly, and one that is proud, lies in this – the one thinks justly of himself, and the other unjustly. The most humble Christian only thinks of himself *soberly, as he ought to think,* (*Romans 12:3*). All the instances of humility recorded of the godly, in the Scriptures, are but so many examples of a *right spirit*, a spirit brought down to their situation. *Carry back the ark of God into the city,* says David: *If I shall find favour in the eyes of the Lord, he will bring me again, and show me both it, and his habitation: but if he thus say, I have no delight in thee; behold, here am I, let him do to me as seemeth good unto him.* (*1 Samuel 15:25, 26*). This was very different from the spirit of his predecessor, when he was given to expect the loss of the kingdom; yet it was no more than was the duty of Saul, as well as of David; and all his proud and rebellious opposition served only to increase his guilt and misery. The spirit of the publican was no more than was becoming a sinner, and would have been becoming in the Pharisee himself.

Finally: If whatever has the promise of spiritual blessings be a spiritual exercise, everything that is *right*, or which *accords with the divine precept*, must be so; for the Scriptures uniformly promise eternal life to every such exercise. They that *do good* shall come forth to the resurrection of life. He that *doeth righteousness* is *righteous*. The giving of *a cup of cold water* to a disciple of Christ, because he belongs to him, will be followed with a disciple's reward. Nay, a *blessing* is pronounced upon those who are *not offended* in him. But, though these things are spiritual, and are characteristic of the godly, yet, who will say they are not binding on the ungodly? Are they excused from *good*, from *doing right*, from bestowing *a cup of water* on a disciple of Jesus, because he belongs to him? At least, are they allowed to be *offended* in him?

If God's law be spiritual, and remain in full force as a standard of obligation; if men, while unconverted, have no real conformity to it; if regeneration be the writing of it upon the heart, or the renewal of the mind to a right spirit; all these things are clear and consistent. This is for the same thing, in different respects, to be "man's duty, and God's gift;" a position which Dr Owen has fully established;[8] and somewhere remarks, that he who is ignorant of it has yet to learn one of the first principles of religion. In short, this is rendering the work of the Spirit what the Scriptures denominate it – LEADING

---

8. *Display of Arminianism*, chapter 10.

US BY THE WAY THAT WE SHOULD GO. (*Isaiah 48:17*). But, if that which is bestowed by the Holy Spirit be something different in its nature from that which is required in the divine precepts, I see not what is to be made of the Scriptures, nor how it is, that *righteousness, goodness*, or anything else which is required of men, should be accompanied, as it is, with the promise of eternal life.

3
Answers to Objections

THE principal objections that are made to the foregoing statement of things, are taken from the nature of original holiness, as it existed in our first parents – The divine decrees – Particular redemption – The covenant of works – The inability of man – The operations of the Spirit – and the necessity of a divine principle in order to believing.

It may be worthy of some notice, at least from those who are perpetually reproaching the statement here defended as leading to Arminianism, that the greater part of these objections are of *Arminian* origin. They are the same for substance as have been alleged by the leading writers of that scheme, in their controversies with the Calvinists; and from the writings of the latter it were easy to select answers to them. This, in effect, is acknowledged by Mr Brine, who, however, considers these answers as insufficient, and therefore prefers others before them. [1]

It also deserves to be considered, whether objections drawn from such subjects as the above, in which we may presently get beyond our depth, ought to weigh against that body of evidence which has been adduced from the plain declarations and precepts of the holy Scriptures? What if by reason of darkness we could not ascertain the precise nature of the principle of our first parents? It is certain we know but little of original purity. Our disordered souls are incapable of forming just ideas of so glorious a state. To attempt,

---

1. *A Refutation of Arminian Principles*, page 6.

therefore, to settle the boundaries of even *their* duty, by an abstract inquiry into the nature of their powers and principles, would be improper; and still more so to make it the medium by which to judge of *our own*. There are but two ways by which we can judge on such a subject: The one is from the *character of the Creator*, and the other from *Scripture testimony*. From the former, we may infer the *perfect purity* of the creature, as coming out of the hands of God; but nothing can be concluded of his inability to believe in Christ, had he been in circumstances which required it. As to the latter, the only passage that I recollect to have seen produced for the purpose, is *1 Corinthians 15:47. The first man was of the earth, earthy*, which Mr Johnson of Liverpool alleged to prove the earthiness of Adam's mind, or principles: but Mr Brine sufficiently refutes this: proving that this divine proposition respects the *body*, and not the principles of our first father; [2] and thus Dr Gill expounds it.

With regard to the doctrine of *divine decrees*, and so on, it is a fact that the great body of the divines who have believed those doctrines, have also believed the other. Neither Augustine, nor Calvin, who each in his day defended predestination, and the other doctrines connected with it, ever appear to have thought of denying it to be the duty of every sinner who has heard the gospel, to repent, and believe in Jesus Christ. Neither did the other reformers, nor the Puritans of the sixteenth century, nor the divines of the Synod of Dort, who opposed Arminius, nor any of the nonconformists of the seventeenth century, so far as I have any acquaintance with their writings, ever so much as hesitate upon this subject. The writings of Calvin himself would now be deemed Arminian by a great number of our opponents. I allow that the principles here defended may be inconsistent with the doctrine of grace notwithstanding the leading advocates of those doctrines have admitted them; and am far from wishing any person to build his faith on the authority of great men: but their admission of them ought to suffice for the silencing of that kind of opposition against them which consists in calling names.

Were a difficulty allowed to exist, as to the reconciling of these subjects, it would not warrant a rejection of either of them. If I find two doctrines affirmed, or implied in the Scriptures, which to my feeble understanding may seem to clash, I ought not to embrace the

---

2. Johnson's *Mistakes noted and rectified*, pages 18-23.

one, and to reject the other, because of their supposed inconsistency: for on the same ground another person might embrace that which I reject, and reject that which I embrace, and have equal *scriptural authority* for his faith, as I have for mine. Yet in this manner many have acted on both sides: some taking the general precepts and invitations of Scripture for their standard, have rejected the doctrine of discriminating grace; others taking the declarations of salvation as being a fruit of electing love, for their standard, deny that sinners without distinction are called upon to believe for the salvation of their souls. Hence it is that we hear of *Calvinistic*, and *Arminian texts;* as though these leaders had agreed to divide the Scriptures between them. The truth is, there are but two ways for us to take: one is to reject them *both*, and the Bible with them, on account of its inconsistencies; or embrace them both, concluding that as they are both revealed in the Scriptures, they are both true, and both consistent, and that it is owing to the darkness of *our* understandings that they do not appear so to us. Those excellent lines of Dr Watts, in his Hymn on Election, one should think, must approve themselves to every pious heart:

> "But, O my soul, if truth so bright
> Should dazzle, and confound thy sight;
> Yet still his written will obey,
> And wait the great decisive day."

Had we more of that, about which we contend, it would teach us more to suspect our own understandings, and to submit to the wisdom of God. Abraham, that pattern of faith, might have made objections to the command of offering up his son, on the ground of its inconsistency with the promise, and might have set himself to find some other meaning for the terms: but he *believed God*, and left it to him to reconcile his promise and his precepts. It was for him not to dispute, but to obey.

These general remarks, however, are not introduced for the purpose of avoiding a particular attention to the several objections, but rather as preparatory to it.

On the Principle of Holiness Possessed by Man in Innocence

THE objection drawn from this subject has been stated in the following words: – "The holy principle connatural to Adam, and concreated with him, was not suited to live unto God through a Mediator; that kind of life was above the extent of his powers, though perfect; and therefore as he in a state of integrity had not a capacity of living unto God, agreeably to the nature of the new covenant; it is apprehended that his posterity, while under the *first* covenant, are not commanded to live unto God in that sort, or in other words, to live by faith on God through a Mediator." [3]

The whole weight of these important conclusions rests upon the two first sentences, and which are mere unfounded assertions. For the truth of them no *proof* whatever is offered. What evidence is there that "the principle of holiness concreated with Adam was not suited to live unto God through a Mediator"? That his circumstances were such as not to need a Mediator, is true; but this involves no such consequence. A subject, while he preserves his loyalty, needs no Mediator in approaching the throne; if he have offended, it is otherwise: but a change of circumstances would not require a change of principles. On the contrary, the same principle of loyal affection that would induce him while innocent to approach the throne with modest confidence, would induce him, after having offended, to approach it with penitence, or, which is the same thing, to be sorry at heart for what he had done: and if a Mediator were at hand, with whose interposition the sovereign had declared himself well pleased, it would at the same time lead him to implore forgiveness in his name.

Had Cain lived before the fall, God would not have been offended at his bringing an offering without a sacrifice; but after that event, and the promise of the woman's seed together with the institution of sacrifices, such a conduct was highly offensive. It was equally disregarding the threatening and the promise: treating the first as if nothing was meant by it; and the last as a matter of no account. It was practically saying, 'God is not in earnest. There is no great evil in sin; nor any necessity for an atonement. If I come with my offering, I shall doubtless be accepted, and my Creator will think himself honoured.' – Such is still the language of a self-righteous heart. But is it thus that Adam's posterity while "under the first covenant," (or rather, while vainly hoping for the promise of the first covenant, after having broken its conditions) are required to approach an offended God? If the principle of Adam in innocence was not suited to live to

3. Mr Brine's *Motives to Love and Unity*, pages 50. 51.

God through a Mediator, and this be the standard of duty to his carnal descendants, it must of course be their duty either not to worship God at all, or to worship him as Cain did, without any respect to an atoning sacrifice. On the contrary, is there not reason to conclude that the case of Cain and Abel was designed to teach mankind, from the very outset of the world, God's determination to have no fellowship with sinners, except through a Mediator; and that all attempts to approach him in any other way would be vain and presumptuous?

It is true that man in innocence was unable to repent of sin, or to believe in the Saviour: for he had no sin to repent of, nor was any Saviour revealed, or needed. But he was equally unable to repent with such a *natural* sorrow for sin as is allowed to be the duty of his posterity, or to believe the history of the gospel in the way which is also allowed to be binding on all who hear it. To this it might be added, he was unable to perform the duty of a father; for he had no children to educate: nor could he pity or relieve the miserable; for there were no miserable objects to be pitied or relieved. Yet we do not conclude from hence that his descendants are excused from these duties.

"That Adam in a state of innocence," says Dr Gill, "had the power of believing in Christ, and did believe in him as the second person of the trinity, as the Son of God, cannot well be denied; since, with the other two persons, he was his creator and preserver. AND HIS NOT BELIEVING IN HIM AS THE MEDIATOR, SAVIOUR, AND REDEEMER, DID NOT ARISE FROM ANY DEFECT OF POWER IN HIM, BUT FROM THE STATE, CONDITION, AND SITUATION IN WHICH HE WAS, AND FROM THE NATURE OF THE REVELATION MADE UNTO HIM; for no doubt Adam had a power to believe every word of God, or any revelation that was or might be made unto him."[4]

Dr Owen, in his *Display of Arminianism*,[5] complains of the attempts of the Arminians to 'draw down our first parents, even from the instant of their forming, into the same condition wherein we are engaged by reason of corrupted nature.' He mentions several of their maxims and sentiments, and among others, two of their sayings, the one, of the *Remonstrants* in their apology, and the other, of the six Arminian collocutors at the Hague. 'The will of man,' say

---

4. *The Cause of God and Truth*, Part III, chapter 3.

5. *Display of Arminianism*, chapter 8.

the former 'had never any spiritual endowments.' 'In the spiritual death of sin,' say the latter, 'there are no spiritual gifts properly wanting in will, because they were never there.' 'The sum is,' adds the Doctor, ironically, speaking their language, 'man was created with a nature, not only weak and imperfect, unable by its native strength and endowments to attain that *supernatural* end for which he was made, and which he was commanded to seek, but depraved also with a love and desire of things repugnant to the will of God, by reason of an inbred inclination to sinning. It does not properly belong to this place to show how they extenuate those gifts also with which they cannot deny but that he was endued, and also deny those which he had; as *a power to believe in Christ*, or to assent unto any truth that God should reveal unto him: and yet they grant this privilege unto every one of his posterity, in that depraved condition of nature, whereinto by sin he cast himself and us. We have all now, they tell, us, a power of believing in Christ, that is, Adam, by his fall, obtained a supernatural endowment, far more excellent than any he had before!'

It is freely allowed that the principle in innocent Adam differed in many *circumstances* from that in believers. The production of the one was a *necessary* act in God, the other *sovereign*. If he would create Adam, his nature required that he should create him *holy*; but he is under no necessity of nature to produce a holy principle in a lapsed creature. The one was left to the choice of its subject to keep it in being; the other is not. The one was exercised in contemplating and adoring God in all his glorious perfections, as displayed in the works of Creation and Providence; the other contemplates and adores him not only in these characters, but as the God of sovereign saving grace. But as these differences lie not in the *nature* of the principle, but are merely *circumstantial*, they make nothing in circumscribing present duty.

That the principle of holiness in Adam, and that which is wrought in believers are *essentially* the same, I conclude from the following reasons.

First, They are both formed after the same likeness; THE IMAGE OF GOD. – *God created man in his own image, in the image of God created he him* – PUT YE *on the new man, which,* AFTER GOD, *is created in righteousness and true holiness. (Genesis 1:27; Ephesians 4:24).*

If God be immutable in his nature, that which is created after him must be the same for substance at all times, and in all circumstances. There cannot be two specifically different images of the same original.

Secondly, They are both a conformity to the same standard; THE MORAL LAW. – That the spirit and conduct of man in innocence was neither more nor less than a perfect conformity to this law, I suppose will be allowed; and the same may be said of the spirit and conduct of Jesus Christ, *so far as he was our exemplar*, or the model after which we are formed. God's law was within his heart. It was *his meat and drink to do his will*. He went to *the end of the law for righteousness;* but it does not appear that he went beyond it. The superiority of his obedience to that of all others, lay not in his doing more than the law required; but in the dignity of his person, which stamped infinite value on everything he did. But if such was the spirit and conduct of Christ, to whose image we are predestinated to be conformed, of necessity it must be ours. This also perfectly agrees with those scriptural representations, which describe the work of the Spirit as *writing God's law in the heart, (Psalm 40:8; John 4:34; Romans 10:4; Jeremiah 31:33*); and those which represent the ultimate state of holiness to which we shall arrive in heaven, as no more than a conformity to this law, and this model: *the spirits of just men* MADE PERFECT ... We shall be LIKE HIM.

Thirdly, The terms used to describe the one imply that it is of the same nature as the other. – Conversion is expressed by a *return* to God, (*Isaiah 55:7*); which denotes a recovery to a right state of mind after a departure from him. Regeneration is called a *washing*, which expresses the restoring of the soul to purity, from which it had degenerated: and hence the same divine operation is in the same passage called, the *renewing* of the Holy Ghost.

But, "this renovation, it has been said, is spoken of the mind, and not of a principle in the mind."[6] The renewal of the mind, must either be natural or moral. If the former, it would seem as if we had divested ourselves of the use of our natural faculties, and that regeneration consists in restoring them. If the latter, by the mind must be meant the *disposition* of the mind, or, as the Scripture speaks, *the* SPIRIT *of our minds. (Ephesians 4:23*). But this amounts to the same

---

6. *Motives to Love and Unity*, page 23.

thing as a principle in our minds. There is no difference between a mind being restored to a right state and condition, and a right state and condition being restored to the mind.

Fourthly, Supreme love to God, which is acknowledged to be the principle of man in innocence, would necessarily lead a fallen creature to embrace the gospel way of salvation. – This is clearly intimated in our Lord's reasonings with the Jews: *I know you, that ye have not the love of God in you. I am come in my Father's name, and ye receive me not. (John 5:42, 43).* This reasoning, on the contrary hypothesis, was invalid; for if receiving the Messiah was that to which a principle of supreme love to God was unequal, a non-reception of him would afford no proof of its absence. They might have had the love of God in them, and yet not have received him.

Love to God, which was possessed by Adam in innocence, was equal to that of the holy angels. His being of the *earth, earthy,* as to his body, no more proves his inferiority to them as to the principles of his mind, than it proves the inferiority of Christ in this respect, who, before his resurrection, was possessed of a natural and not a spiritual body. But it cannot be denied that the angels are capable of understanding, believing, and approving of the gospel way of salvation. It is, above all others, their chosen theme: *which things the angels desire to look into. (1 Peter 1:12).* It is true, they do not embrace the Messiah *as their Saviour;* because they do not stand in need of salvation; but give a being that wants a Saviour, a free invitation, and their principles, and he would not scruple a moment about accepting it. It is not possible for a creature to love God, without loving the greatest friend of God, and embracing a gospel that more than anything tends to exalt his character: neither is it possible to love mankind with a holy and affectionate regard towards their best interests, without loving the friend of sinners, and approving of a doctrine that breathes *good will to men.*

Concerning the Decrees of God

A GENERAL invitation to sinners to return to God, and be saved through Christ, it has been thought, must be inconsistent with an election of some, and a consequent rejection of others. Such has been the mode of objecting used by the adversaries to the doctrines of discriminating grace;[7] and such is the mode of late adopted by our opponents.

In general I would observe, If this mode of reasoning proves anything, it will prove too much; it will prove that it is not the duty of some men to attend the means of grace, or in any way to seek after the salvation of their souls, or to be in the least degree concerned about it: for it may be pleaded that God cannot have made it their duty, or have invited them to attend the means of salvation, seeing he is determined not to bestow salvation upon them. And thus we must not only be driven to explain the general invitation, to many who never came to the gospel supper, of a mere invitation to attend the means of grace, but must absolutely give it up, and the Bible with it, on account of its inconsistency.

Further, This mode of reasoning would prove that the use of means in order to obtain a temporal subsistence, and to preserve life, is altogether vain and inconsistent. If we believe that the future states of men are determined of God, we must also believe the same of their present states. The Scriptures teach the one, no less than the other. *God hath determined the times before appointed, and the bounds of our habitation.* Our *cup* is measured, and our *lot* assigned us. There is also *an appointed time for man upon earth: his days are as the days of an hireling. – His days are determined, and the number of his months are with God: He has appointed his bounds that he cannot pass. (Acts 17:26; Psalm 16:5; Job 7:1; 14:5).* Yet those who reason as above, with regard to things of another life, are as attentive to the affairs of *this* life as other people. They are no less concerned than their neighbours for their present accommodation; nor less employed in devising means for the lengthening out of their lives, and of their tranquillity. But if the purpose of God is compatible with the agency of man in present concerns, it may in those which are future, whether we can perceive the link that unites them or not: and if our duty in the one case be the same as if no such purpose existed, it is so in the other. *Secret things belong unto the Lord our God: but those things which are revealed belong unto us and to our children for ever. (Deuteronomy 29:29).*

It was the duty of Pharaoh to have followed the counsel of Moses, and to have let the people go; and his sin to pursue them into the sea: yet it was the purpose of God by this means to destroy him,

---

7. See Owen's *Death of Death*, Book IV. Chapter 1.

(*Exodus 7:1-4*); *Moses sent messengers to Sihon king of Heshbon with words of peace, saying, Let me pass through thy land;* and it was doubtless the duty of Sihon to have complied with the request: yet it appears by the issue that the Lord had determined to give his country to Israel for a possession, and therefore gave him up to hardness of heart, by which it was accomplished. (*Deuteronomy 2:26-30*).

If the days of man are determined, and his bounds appointed that he cannot pass them, it must have been determined that that generation of the Israelites who went out of Egypt should die in the wilderness: yet it was their duty to have believed God, and to have gone up to possess the land; and their sin to disbelieve him, and turn back in their hearts to Egypt. And it deserves particular notice, that this their sin is held up, both by David and Paul, as an example for others to shun, and that in spiritual concerns. (*1 Corinthians 10:6-12*). It was the determination of God that Ahab should fall in his expedition against Ramoth Gilead, as was plainly intimated to him by Micaiah: yet it was his duty to have hearkened to the counsel that was given him, and to have desisted from his purpose. (*1 Kings 22:15-22*). The destruction of Jerusalem by the Chaldeans was determined of God, and frequently foretold by the prophets: yet the inhabitants were as frequently counselled to return from their evil ways that they might avoid it. Jeremiah particularly entreated Zedekiah to follow his counsel, that he might save the city and himself from ruin. (*Jeremiah 38:20*).

However such things may grate upon the minds of some, yet there are cases in which we ourselves are in the habit of using similar language, and that without any idea of attributing to God anything inconsistent with the greatest perfection of moral character. If a wicked man be set on mischievous pursuits, and all the advice and warnings of his friends be lost upon him, we do not scruple to say, 'It seems as if God had determined to destroy him, and therefore has given him up to infatuation.' In the use of such language we have no idea of the determination of God being unjust, or capricious. On the contrary, we suppose he may have *wise* and *just* reasons for doing as he does; and as such, notwithstanding our compassion towards the party, we acquiesce in it. Whenever we speak of God as having determined to destroy a person, or a people, we feel the subject too profound for our comprehension; and well indeed we may.

Even an inspired apostle, when discoursing of God's rejection of the Jewish nation, though he glances at the merciful aspect which this awful event wore towards the Gentiles, and traces some great and wise designs that should be answered by it; yet feels himself lost in his subject. Standing as on the brink of an unfathomable abyss, he exclaims, *O the depth of the riches both of the wisdom and knowledge of God! how unsearchable are his judgments, and his ways past finding out! (Romans 11:33).* He believed the doctrine of divine decrees, or that God *worketh all things after the counsel of his own will:* but he had no idea of making these things any part of the rule of duty; either so as to excuse his countrymen from the sin of unbelief, or himself from using every possible means that might accomplish their salvation. On the one hand, he quoted the words of David as applicable to them. *Let their table be made a snare, and a trap, and a stumbling-block, and a recompense unto them.* On the other, he declares, *I speak to you Gentiles ... if by* ANY MEANS *I may provoke to emulation them which are my flesh, and might save some of them. (Romans 11:9, 13, 14).*

There were those in that day, as well as in this, who objected, that if things be as God hath purposed, *Why doth he yet find fault? For who hath resisted his will? (Romans 9:19).* This was nothing other than suggesting that the doctrine of decrees must needs operate to the setting aside of the fault of sinners; and this is the substance of what has been alleged from that day to this. Some, because they cannot conceive of the doctrine but as drawing after it the consequence assigned to it by this *replier against God*, reject it; others appear to have no objection to the consequence itself, stamped as it is with infamy by the manner in which the apostle repelled it, and therefore admit the doctrine as connected with it! But Paul did not do so. He held fast the doctrine of decrees, and held it as comporting with the *fault* of sinners. After all that he had written upon God's electing some, and rejecting others – he in the same chapter assigns the failure of those that failed, to their *not seeking justification by faith in Christ; but as it were by the works of the law, stumbling at the stumbling-stone. (Romans 9:32).*

"God's Word," says Mr Brine, "and not his secret purpose, is the rule of our conduct."[8] "We must exactly distinguish," says Dr Owen, "between man's duty, and God's purpose; there being no connection

---

8. *Certain Efficacy*, etc. page 151.

between them. The purpose and decree of God is not the rule of our duty; neither is the performance of our duty, in doing what we are commanded, any declaration of what is God's purpose to do, or his decree that it should be done. Especially is this to be seen and considered in the duty of the ministers of the gospel; in the dispensing of the Word, in exhortations, invitations, precepts, and threatenings, committed unto them; all of which are perpetual declaratives of our duty; and do manifest the approbation of the thing exhorted and invited to, with the truth of the connection between one thing and another; but not of the counsel or purpose of God, in respect of individual persons, in the ministry of the Word. A minister is not to make inquiry after, nor to trouble himself about, those secrets of the eternal mind of God, – whom he purposeth to save, and whom he hath sent Christ to die for in particular, – it is enough for them to search his revealed will; and thence take their *directions*, from whence they have their *commissions*. Wherefore, there is no conclusion from the universal precepts of the Word, concerning the things relating to God's purpose in himself concerning persons: they command and invite all to *repent* and *believe:* but they know not in particular on whom God will bestow repentance unto salvation, nor in whom he will effect the work of faith with power." [9]

On Particular Redemption

OBJECTIONS to the foregoing principles from the doctrine of election are generally united with those from particular redemption: and indeed they are so connected that the validity of the one stands or falls with that of the other.

To ascertain the force of the objection, it is proper to enquire, wherein the peculiarity of redemption consists? If the atonement of Christ were considered as the literal payment of a debt; if the measure of his sufferings were according to the number of those for whom he died, and to the degree of their guilt, in such a manner as that if more had been saved, or if those who are saved had been more guilty, his sorrows must have been proportionably increased, it might, for anything I know, be inconsistent with indefinite invitations. But it would be equally inconsistent with the free *forgiveness* of sin, and with sinners being directed to apply for mercy as *supplicants*,

---

9. *Death of Death*, Book IV, chapter 1.

rather than as *claimants*. I conclude, therefore, that a hypothesis which in so many important points is manifestly inconsistent with the Scriptures, cannot be true.

On the other hand, if the atonement of Christ proceed not on the principle of commercial, but of moral justice, or justice as it relates to *crime;* if its grand object were to express the divine displeasure against sin, (*Romans 8:3*), and so to render the exercise of mercy, in all the ways wherein sovereign wisdom should determine to apply it, consistent with righteousness, (*Romans 3:26*); if it be in itself equal to the salvation of the whole world, were the whole world to embrace it; and if the peculiarity which attends it, consist not in its insufficiency to save more than are saved, but in the sovereignty of its application, no such inconsistency can justly be ascribed to it.

If the atonement of Christ excluded a part of mankind *in the same sense* as it excludes fallen angels, why is the gospel addressed to the one, any more than to the other? The message of wisdom is addressed to men, and not to devils. The former are invited to the gospel supper, but the latter are not. These facts afford proof that Christ by his death opened a door of hope to sinners of the human race *as sinners; affording a basis for their being invited without distinction to believe and be saved.*

But as God might send his Son into the world to save men, rather than angels; so he may *apply* his sacrifice to the salvation of some men, and not of others. It is a fact that a great part of the world have never heard the gospel; that the greater part of those who *have* heard it, disregard it; and that those who believe are taught to ascribe not only their salvation, but faith itself, through which it is obtained, to the *free gift of God.* And as the application of redemption is solely directed by sovereign wisdom; so, like every other event, it is the result of *previous design.* That which is actually done was *intended* to be done. Hence the salvation of those that are saved is described as the *end* which the Saviour had in view: *He gave himself for us, that he might redeem us from all iniquity, and purify unto himself a peculiar people, zealous of good works.* (*Titus 2:14*). Herein, it is apprehended, consists the peculiarity of redemption.

There is no contradiction between this peculiarity of *design* in the death of Christ, and a universal obligation on those who hear the gospel, to believe in him, or a universal invitation being addressed to them. If God through the death of his Son has promised salvation to all who comply with the gospel; and if there be no *natural* impossibility as to a compliance, nor any obstruction but that which arises from aversion of heart; exhortations and invitations to believe and be saved, are consistent. And our duty as preachers of the gospel is to administer them, without any more regard to particular redemption than to election; both being secret things which belong to the Lord our God, and which, however they be a rule to him, are none to us. If that which sinners are called upon to believe respected the particular design of Christ to save them, it would then be inconsistent: but they are neither exhorted nor invited to believe anything but what is revealed, and what will prove true, whether they believe it or not. He that believeth in Jesus Christ, must believe in him as he is revealed in the gospel; and that is as the Saviour of *sinners*. It is only *as a sinner*, exposed to the righteous displeasure of God, that he must approach him. If he thinks of coming to him as a favourite of heaven, or as possessed of any good qualities which may recommend him before other sinners, he deceives his soul: such notions are the bar to believing. "He that will know his own particular redemption, before he will believe," says a well-known writer, "begins at the wrong end of his work, and is very unlikely to come that way to the knowledge of it. – Any man that owns himself a *sinner*, hath as fair a ground for his faith as anyone in the world that hath not yet believed; nor may any person on any account exclude himself from redemption, unless by his obstinate and resolved continuance in unbelief, he hath marked out himself." [10]

"The preachers of the gospel, in their particular congregations," says another, "being utterly unacquainted with the purpose, and secret counsel of God, being also forbidden to pray or search into it, (*Deuteronomy 29:29*), may justifiably call upon every man to believe, with assurance of salvation to every one in particular upon his so doing; knowing, and being fully persuaded of this, that there is enough in the death of Christ to save every one that shall do so: leaving the purpose and counsel of God, on whom he will bestow faith, and for whom in particular Christ died, (even as they are commanded) to himself." – When God calls upon men to believe, he does not, in the first place, call upon them to believe that Christ died

---

10. Elisha Coles on *God's Sovereignty*, on Redemption.

for them; but that *there is none other name under heaven given among men, whereby we must be saved*, but only of *Jesus Christ*, through whom salvation is preached." [11]

On Sinners being Under the Covenant of Works

MUCH has been said on this subject in relation to the present controversy. [12] Yet I feel at a loss in forming a judgment wherein the force of the objection lies, as it is nowhere, that I recollect, formed into a regular argument. If I understand Mr Brine, he supposes, *First*, That all duty is required by the law, either as a rule of life, or as a covenant. *Secondly*, That all unconverted sinners, being under the law as a covenant, whatever the revealed will of God now requires of them, it is to be considered as the requirement of that covenant. *Thirdly*, That the terms of the covenant of works being, *do and live*, it cannot for this reason be, *believe and be saved*.

But allowing the distinction between the law as a rule of life, and as a covenant, to be just; before any conclusion can be drawn from it, it requires to be ascertained in what sense unbelievers are under a covenant of works; and whether in some respects it be not their sin to continue so? That they are *under the curse* for having broken it, is true; and that they are still labouring to substitute something in the place of perfect obedience, by which they may regain the divine favour, is true also; but *this latter ought not to be*. A self-righteous attachment to a covenant of works, or, as the Scripture expresses it, a being *of the works of the law*, is no other than the working of unbelief, and rebellion against the truth. Strictly speaking, men are not now under the covenant of works; but under the *curse* for having broken it. God is not in covenant with them, nor they with him. The law as a covenant was recorded, and a new and enlarged edition of it given to Israel at Mount Sinai; not however for the purpose of *giving life* to those who had broken it; but rather as a preparative to a better covenant. Its *precepts* still stand as the immutable will of God towards his creatures; its *promises* as memorials of what might have been expected from his goodness in case of obedience; and its *curses* as a flaming sword that guards the tree of life. It is stationed in the oracles of God as a faithful watchman to repel the vain hopes of

---

11. Dr Owen's *Death of Death*, Book IV, chapter 1.

12. *Motives to Love and Unity*, pages 37-43.

the self-righteous, and convince them of the necessity of a Saviour. (*Romans 7:10; Matthew 19:17*). Hence it was given to Israel by the hand of Moses *as a Mediator*. See *Galatians 3:19-21*.

But if unbelievers be no otherwise under the covenant of works than as they are exposed to its curse, it is improper to say, that whatever is required of them in the Scriptures, is required by that covenant, and as a term of life, God requires nothing of fallen creatures, as *a term of life*. He requires them to love him with all their hearts, the same as if they had never apostatised; but not with a view to regain his lost favour; for were they henceforward perfectly to comply with the divine precepts, unless they could atone for past offences, which is impossible, they could have no ground to expect the bestowment of everlasting life. It is enough for us that the revealed will of God to sinners, says *believe;* while the gospel graciously adds the promise of *salvation*.

On the Inability of Sinners to Believe in Christ and Do things Spiritually Good

THIS objection is seldom explicitly stated, unless it be by persons who deny it to be the duty of a sinner to love God with all his heart, and his neighbour as himself. Intimations are often given, however, that it is absurd and cruel to require of any man what is beyond his power to comply with; and as the Scriptures declare that, *No man* CAN *come to Christ, except the Father draw him; and that the natural man receiveth not the things of the Spirit of God, neither* CAN *he know them, because they are spiritually discerned;* it is concluded that these are things to which the sinner, while unregenerate, is under no obligation. (*John 6:44; 1 Corinthians 2:14*).

The answer that has frequently been made to this reasoning is, in effect, as follows: 'Men are no more unable to do things spiritually good, than they are to be subject to the law of God, which *the carnal mind is not, nor* CAN *be*. And the reason why we have no power to comply with these things is, we have lost it by the fall: but though we have lost our ability to obey, God has not lost his authority to command.' There is some truth in this answer; but it is apprehended to be insufficient. It is true that sinners are no more, and no otherwise unable to do anything spiritually good, than they are to yield a perfect submission to God's holy law; and that the inability of both arises from the same source – the original apostasy of human nature. Yet if the nature of this inability were direct, or such as consisted in the want of *rational faculties, bodily powers, or external advantages;* its being the consequence of the fall, would not set aside the objection. Some men pass through life totally insane. This may be one of the *effects* of sin; yet the Scriptures never convey any idea of such persons being dealt with at the last judgment on the same ground as if they had been sane. On the contrary, they teach that *to whom much is given, of him much shall be required. (Luke 12:48)*. Another is deprived of the sight of his eyes, and so rendered unable to read the Scriptures. This also may be the *effect* of sin; and, in some cases, of his own personal misconduct: but whatever punishment may be inflicted on him for such misconduct, he is not blameworthy for not reading the Scriptures, after he had lost his ability for doing so. A third possesses the use of reason, and of all his senses, and members; but has no other opportunity of knowing the will of God than what is afforded him by the light of nature. It would be equally repugnant to Scripture and reason to suppose that this man will be judged by the same rule as others who have lived under the light of revelation. *As many as have sinned without law shall also perish without law: and as many as have sinned in the law shall be judged by the law. (Romans 2:12)*.

The inability in each of these cases is *natural;* and to whatever degree it exists, let it arise from what cause it may, it excuses the subject of blame, in the account of both God and man. The law of God itself requires no creature to love him, or obey him, beyond his *strength*, or with more than all the powers which he possesses. If the inability of sinners to believe in Christ, or to do things spiritually good, were of this nature, it would undoubtedly form an excuse in their favour; and it must be as absurd to exhort them to such duties, as to exhort the blind to look. the deaf to hear, or the dead to walk. But the inability of sinners is not such as to induce the Judge of all the earth, (who cannot do other than right), to abate in his requirements. It is a fact that he does require them, – and that without paying any regard to their inability, – *to love him*, and *to fear him*, and *to do all his commandments always. The blind* are admonished, *to look, the deaf to hear*, and *the dead to arise. (Isaiah 42:18; Ephesians 5:14)*. If there were no other proof than what is afforded by this single fact, it ought to satisfy us that the blindness, deafness, and death of sinners, to that which is spiritually good, is of a different nature from that which furnishes an excuse. This however is not the only ground of proof. The thing speaks for itself. There is an essential difference between an inability which is independent of the inclination, and one that is owing to nothing else. It is equally impossible, no doubt, for any person to do that which he has no mind to do, as to perform that which surpasses his natural powers; and hence it is that the same terms are used in the one case as in the other. Those who were under the dominion of envy and malignity, COULD NOT *speak peaceably;* and those who have *eyes full of adultery,* CANNOT *cease from sin.* Hence also the following language – *How* CAN *ye, being evil, speak good things?* – *The natural man receiveth not the things of the Spirit of God: neither* CAN *he know them.* – *The carnal mind is enmity against God: for it is not subject to the law of God, neither indeed* CAN *be. So then they that are in the flesh* CANNOT *please God.* – *No man* CAN *come to me, except the Father who sent me draw him.* (*1 Corinthians 2:14; Romans 8:7, 8; John 6:44*). It is also true, that many have affected to treat the distinction between natural and moral inability as more curious than solid. 'If we be unable,' say they, 'we are unable. As to the nature of the inability, it is a matter of no account. Such distinctions are perplexing to plain Christians, and beyond their capacity.' But surely the plainest and weakest Christian in reading his Bible, if he pays any regard to what he reads; must perceive a manifest difference between the blindness of Bartimeus, who was ardently desirous that *he might receive his sight;* and that of the unbelieving Jews, who *closed their eyes, lest they should see, and be converted, and healed,* (*Mark 10:51; Matthew 13:15*); and between the want of the natural sense of hearing, and the state of those *who have ears, but hear not.*

So far as my observation extends, those persons who affect to treat this distinction as a matter of mere curious speculation, are as ready to make use of it as other people where their own interest is concerned. If they be accused of injuring their fellow-creatures, and can allege that what they did was not *knowingly,* or of *design,* I believe they never fail to do so: or when charged with neglecting their duty to a parent, or a master; if they can say in truth that they were *unable* to do it at the time, *let their will have been ever so good,* they are never known to omit the plea: and should such a master or parent reply by suggesting that their want of ability arose from want of *inclination*, they would very easily understand it to be the language of reproach, and be very earnest to maintain the contrary. You never hear a person, in such circumstances, reason as he does in religion. He does not say, 'If I be unable, I am unable; it is of no account whether it be of this kind or that;' but labours with all his might to establish the difference. Now if the subject be so clearly understood and acted upon where interest is concerned, and never appears difficult but in religion, it is but too manifest where the difficulty lies. If by fixing the guilt of our conduct upon our father Adam, we can sit comfortably in our nest; we shall be very averse to a sentiment that tends to disturb our repose, by planting a thorn in it.

It is sometimes objected, that the inability of sinners to believe in Christ is not the effect of their depravity; on the basis that Adam himself in his purest state was only a *natural man*, and had no power to perform spiritual duties. But this objection belongs to another topic, and has, I hope, been already answered. To this, however, it may be added – *The natural man* who *receiveth not the things of the spirit of God*, (*1 Corinthians 2:14*), is not a man possessed of the holy image of God, as was Adam, but of mere natural accomplishments; as were the *wise men of the world*, the philosophers of Greece and Rome, to whom the things of God were *foolishness*. Moreover, if the inability of sinners to perform spiritual duties were of the kind alleged in the objection, they must be equally unable to commit the opposite sins. He that from the constitution of his nature is absolutely unable to understand, or believe, or love a certain kind of truth, must of necessity be alike unable to *shut his eyes* against it, to disbelieve, to reject, or to hate it. But it is manifest that all men are capable of the latter; it must therefore follow that nothing but the depravity of their hearts renders them incapable of the former.

Some writers, as has been already observed, have allowed that sinners are the subjects of an inability which arises from their depravity; but they still contend that this is not *all;* but that they are both *naturally* and *morally* unable to believe in Christ; and this they think agreeable to the Scriptures, which represent them as both *unable* and *unwilling* to come to him for life. But these two kinds of inability cannot consist with each other, so as both to exist in the same subject, and towards the same thing. A moral inability *supposes* a natural ability. He who never in any state was possessed of the power of seeing, cannot be said to *shut his eyes* against the light. If the Jews had not been possessed of natural powers, equal to the knowledge of Christ's doctrine, there had been no justice in that cutting question, and answer, *Why do ye not understand my speech? Because ye* CANNOT *hear my word*. A total physical inability must of necessity supersede a moral one. To suppose, therefore, that the phrase, *No man* CAN *come to me*, is meant to describe the former; and, *Ye* WILL NOT *come to me that ye may have life*, the latter; is to suppose that our Saviour taught what is self-contradictory.

Some have supposed that in ascribing physical or natural power to men, we deny their *natural depravity*. Through the poverty of language, words are obliged to be used in different senses. When we speak of men as *by nature* depraved, we do not mean to convey the idea of sin being an essential part of human nature, or of the constitution of man as man: our meaning is, that it is not a mere effect of education and example; but is from his very birth so interwoven through all his powers, so ingrained, as it were, in his very soul, as to grow up with him, and become natural to him.

On the other hand, when the term *natural* is used as opposed to *moral*, and applied to the powers of the soul, it is designed to express those faculties which are strictly a part of our nature as men, and which are necessary to our being accountable creatures. By confounding these ideas we may be always disputing, and bring nothing to an issue.

Finally, It is sometimes suggested, that to ascribe natural ability to sinners to perform things spiritually good, is to nourish their self-sufficiency; and that to represent their inability as only *moral*, is to suppose that it is not insuperable, but may after all be overcome by efforts of their own. But surely it is not necessary, in order to destroy a spirit of self-sufficiency, to deny that we are men, and accountable creatures; which is all that natural ability supposes. If any person imagine it possible, of his own accord to choose that to which he is utterly averse, let him make the trial.

Some have alleged that 'natural power is only sufficient to perform natural things; and that spiritual power is required to the performance of spiritual things.' But this statement is far from being accurate.

Natural power is as necessary to the performance of spiritual, as of natural things: we must possess the powers of men in order to perform the duties of good men. And as to spiritual power, or, which is the same thing, a right state of mind, it is not properly a faculty of the soul, but a quality which it possesses: and which though it be essential to the *actual performance* of spiritual obedience, yet is not necessary to our being under *obligation* to perform it.

If a traveller, from an aversion to the western continent, should direct his course perpetually towards the east, he would in time arrive at the place which he designed to shun. In like manner, it has been remarked by some who have observed the progress of this controversy, that, there are certain important points in which false Calvinism, in its ardent desire to steer clear of Arminianism, is brought to agree with it. We have seen already that they agree in their notions of the original holiness in Adam, and the inconsistency of the duty of believing with the doctrine of Election and particular redemption. To this may be added, they are agreed in making the *grace of God* necessary to the accountability of sinners, with regard to spiritual obedience. The one pleads for graceless sinners being free from obligation; the other admits of obligation, but founds it on the notion of universal grace. Both are agreed that, where there is no grace, there can be no duty. But if grace be the ground of obligation, it is no more grace, but debt. It is that which, if anything good be required of the sinner, cannot justly be withheld. This, in effect, is acknowledged by both parties. The one contends that where no grace is given, there can be no obligation to spiritual obedience, and therefore acquits the unbeliever of guilt in not coming to Christ that he might have life, and in the neglect of all spiritual religion. The other argues that if man be totally depraved, and no grace be given him to counteract his depravity, he is blameless: that is, his depravity is no longer depravity: he is innocent in the account of his judge; consequently he can need no Saviour; and if justice be done him, will be exempt from punishment, if not entitled to heaven, in virtue of his personal innocence. Thus the whole system of grace is rendered void; and fallen angels, who have not been partakers of it, must be in a far preferable state to that of fallen men, who, by Jesus taking hold of their nature, are liable to become blameworthy, and eternally lost. But if the essential powers of the mind be the same, whether we be pure or depraved, and be sufficient to render any creature an accountable being, whatever be his disposition, grace is what its proper meaning imports, – *free favour*, or *favour towards the unworthy;* and the redemption of Christ, with all its holy: and happy effects, is what the Scriptures represent it, – *necessary to deliver us from the state into which we were fallen antecedent to its being bestowed.* (*Romans 5:5, 15-21; Hebrews 9:27, 28; 1 Thessalonians 1:10*).

On the Work of the Holy Spirit

THE Scriptures clearly ascribe both repentance and faith, wherever they exist, to divine influence. (*Ezekiel 11:19; 2 Timothy 2:25; Ephesians 1:17; 2:8*). From hence many have concluded that they cannot be duties required of sinners. If sinners have been exhorted from the pulpit to repent or believe, they have thought it sufficient to show the absurdity of such exhortations by saying, 'An heart of flesh is of *God's giving. Faith is not of ourselves; it is the gift of God;*' as though these things were inconsistent, and it were improper to exhort to anything but what can be done of ourselves, and without the influence of the Holy Spirit.

The whole weight of this objection rests upon the supposition, That *we do not stand in need of the Holy Spirit to enable us to comply with our duty.* If this principle were admitted, we must conclude, either with the Arminians and Socinians, that "Faith and conversion, seeing they are acts of obedience, cannot be wrought of God;" [13] or with the objector, that, seeing they *are* wrought of God, they cannot be acts of obedience. But if we need the influence of the Holy Spirit *to enable us to do our duty*, both these methods of reasoning fall to the ground.

And is it not manifest that the godly in all ages have considered themselves as insufficient to perform those things to which, nevertheless, they acknowledge themselves obliged? The rule of duty is what God requires of us: but he requires those things which good men have always confessed themselves, on account of the sinfulness of their nature, insufficient to perform. He *desireth truth in the inward parts;* yet an Apostle acknowledged that they were not sufficient of themselves to *think any thing as of themselves; but their sufficiency was of God.* (*Psalm 51:6; 2 Corinthians 3:5*). *The Spirit,*

---

13. See Owen's *Display of Arminianism,* chapter 10.

saith he, *helpeth our infirmities: for we know not what we should pray for* AS WE OUGHT: *but the Spirit itself maketh intercession for us with groanings which cannot be uttered.* (*Romans 8:26*). The same things are required in one place, which are promised in another: – *Only fear the Lord, and serve him in truth with all your heart. – I will put my fear in their hearts, that they shall not depart from me.* (*1 Samuel 12:24; Jeremiah 32:40*). – When the sacred writers speak of the divine precepts, they neither disown them, nor infer from them a self-sufficiency to conform to them; but turn them into prayer: – *Thou hast* COMMANDED *us to keep thy precepts diligently. Oh that my ways were directed to keep thy statutes!* (*Psalm 119:4, 5*). – In summary, the Scriptures uniformly teach us that all our sufficiency to do good, or to abstain from evil, is from above: repentance and faith, therefore, may be duties, notwithstanding their being the gifts of God.

If our insufficiency for this, and every other good thing, arose from a natural impotency, it would indeed excuse us from obligation: but if it arise from the sinful dispositions of our hearts, it is otherwise. Those whose eyes are *full of adultery, and* THEREFORE *cannot cease from sin*, are under the same obligations to live a chaste and sober life, as other men are: yet if ever their dispositions be changed, it must be by an influence from outside them; for it is not in them to relinquish their courses of their own accord. I do not mean to suggest that this species of evil prevails in all sinners: but sin in some form prevails, and has its dominion over them, and to such a degree that nothing but the grace of God can effectually cure it. It is depravity alone that renders the regenerating influence of the Holy Spirit necessary. "The bare and outward declaration of the Word of God," says a great writer, [14] "ought to have largely sufficed to make it to be believed, if our own blindness and stubbornness did not withstand it. But our mind hath such an inclination to vanity, that it can never cleave fast to the truth of God; and such a dullness, that it is always blind, and cannot see the light thereof, therefore there is nothing available done by the Word, without the enlightening of the Holy Spirit."

On the Necessity of a Divine Principle in Order to Believing

ABOUT fifty years ago, much was written in favour of this position by Mr Brine. Of late years, much has been advanced against it by

---

14. Calvin: See *Institutes*, Book III, chapter 2.

Mr Booth, Mr McLean, and others. I cannot pretend to determine what ideas Mr Brine attached to the term *principle*. He probably meant something different from what God requires of every intelligent creature: and if this were admitted to be necessary to believing, such believing could not be the duty of any, except those who were possessed of it. I have no interest in the question, further than to maintain that, *The moral state, or disposition of the soul, has a necessary influence on believing in Christ.* This I feel no difficulty in admitting on the one side, nor in defending on the other. If faith were an involuntary reception of the truth, and were produced merely by the power of evidence; if the prejudiced or unprejudiced state of the mind had no influence in retarding or promoting it; in essence, if it were wholly an intellectual, and not a moral exercise; then nothing more than rationality, or a capacity of understanding the nature of evidence would be necessary to it. In this case it would not be a *duty;* nor would unbelief be a *sin,* but a mere mistake of the judgement. Nor could there be any need of divine influence: for the special influences of the Holy Spirit are not required for the production of that which has no holiness in it.

But if, on the other hand, faith in Christ be that *on* which the *will* has an influence; if it be the same thing as *receiving the love of the truth, that we may be saved:* if aversion of heart be the only obstruction to it, and the removal of that aversion be the kind of influence necessary to produce it; (and whether these things be so, or not, let the evidence adduced in the second chapter of this treatise determine, [15]) a contrary conclusion must be drawn. The mere force of evidence, however clear, will not change the disposition of the heart. In this case, therefore, and this only, it requires *the exceeding greatness of divine power* to enable a sinner to believe.

But this prompts the *objection* to faith being a duty, and it to this that I now attend. If a sinner cannot believe in Christ, without being renewed in the spirit of his mind, believing, it is suggested, cannot be his *immediate* duty. It is remarkable in how many points the system here opposed agrees with Arminianism. The latter admits believing to be the duty of the unregenerate; but on this account denies the necessity of a divine change in order to it. The former admits the necessity of a divine change in order to believing; but on this account

---

15. Particularly Propositions IV and V.

denies that believing can be the duty of the unregenerate. In this they are agreed, that the necessity of a divine change, and the obligation of the sinner, are not compatible with each other.

But if this argument has any force, it will prove more than its abettors wish it to prove. It will prove that *divine influence* is not necessary to believing: or if it be, that faith *is not the* IMMEDIATE *duty of the sinner*. Whether divine influence changes the bias of the heart in order to believing, or causes us to believe without such change, or only *assists* us in it, makes no difference as to this argument: if it be antecedent, and necessary to believing, believing cannot be a duty, according to the reasoning in the objection, until it is communicated. On this principle, Socinians, who allow faith to be the sinner's *immediate* duty, deny it to be the gift of God. [16]

To me it appears that the necessity of divine influence, and even of a change of heart, prior to believing, is perfectly consistent with its being the immediate duty of the unregenerate. If that disposition of heart which is produced by the Holy Spirit, be *no more than every intelligent creature ought at all times to possess*, the want of it can afford no excuse for the omission of any duty to which it is necessary. Let the contrary supposition be applied to the common affairs of life, and we shall see what work it will make:

> I am not possessed of a principle of common honesty:
> But no man is obliged to exercise a principle which he does
>   not possess:
> Therefore I am not obliged to live in the exercise of common
>   honesty!

While reasoning upon the absence of moral principles, we are exceedingly apt to forget ourselves, and to consider them as a kind of natural accomplishment, which we are not obliged to possess, but merely to improve, in case of being possessed of them; and that, until then, the whole of our duty consists either in *praying* to God to bestow them upon us, or in *waiting* until he shall graciously be pleased to do so. But what should we say, if a man were to reason thus with respect to the common duties of life? Does the whole duty of a dishonest man consist in either *praying* to God to make him honest, or *waiting* until he does so? Everyone in this case feels that an honest heart is *itself* that which he ought to possess. Nor would

---

16. *Narrative of the York Baptists*, Letter 3.

any man, in matters that concerned *his own interest*, think of excusing it, by alleging that the poor man *could not* give it to himself, nor act otherwise than he did, until he possessed it.

If an upright heart towards God and man be not *itself* required of us, nothing is or can be required; for all duty is comprehended in the acting out of the heart. Even those who would compromise the matter by allowing that sinners are not obliged to *possess* an upright heart, but merely to *pray* and *wait* for it; if they would oblige themselves to understand words before they used them, must perceive that there is no meaning in this language. For if it be the duty of a sinner to *pray* to God for an upright heart, and to *wait* for its bestowment, I would enquire, whether these exercises ought to be attended to *sincerely* or *insincerely;* with a true desire after the object sought, or without it? It will not be pretended that he ought to use these means insincerely: but to say he ought to use them sincerely, or with a desire after that for which he prays and waits, is equivalent to saying, he ought to *be sincere;* which is the same thing as possessing an upright heart. If a sinner be destitute of all desire after God, and spiritual things, and set on evil; all the forms into which his duty may be thrown, will make no difference. The carnal heart will meet it in every approach, and repel it. Exhort him to repentance: he tells you that he cannot repent; his heart is too hard to melt, or be in any way affected with his situation. Say, with a certain writer, he ought to *endeavour* to repent: he answers, he has no heart to go about it. Tell him he must pray to God to give him a heart: he replies, prayer is the expression of desire, and I have none to express. What shall we say then? Seeing he cannot repent, cannot find in his heart to *endeavour* to repent, cannot *pray* sincerely for a heart to make such an endeavour; – shall we deny his assertions, and tell him he is not so wicked as he makes himself? – This might be more than we should be able to maintain. – Or shall we allow them, and acquit him of obligation? Rather, ought we not to return to the place where we set out, admonishing him, as the Scriptures direct, to *repent and believe the gospel;* declaring to him that what he calls his inability is his sin, and shame; and warning him against the idea of its availing him another day; not in expectation that of his own accord he may change his mind, but in hope *that God peradventure may give him repentance to the acknowledging of the truth.*

This doctrine, it will be said, must drive sinners to *despair*. Be it so, it is such despair as I wish to see prevail. Until a sinner despairs of any help from himself, he will never fall into the arms of sovereign mercy: but if once we are convinced *that there is no help in us*, and that this is so far from excusing us, that it is a proof of the greatest wickedness, we shall then begin to pray as *lost sinners*, and such prayer offered *in the name of Jesus* will be heard.

Other objections may have been advanced, but I hope it will be allowed that the most important ones have been fairly stated: whether they have been answered, the reader will judge.

Concluding Reflections

FIRST: *Though faith be a duty, the requirement of it is not to be considered as a mere exercise of* AUTHORITY, *but of* INFINITE GOODNESS; *binding us to pursue our best interest.* If a message of peace were sent to a company of rebels, who had been conquered, and lay at the mercy of their injured sovereign, they must, of course, be required to repent, and embrace it, before they could be interested in it; yet such a requirement would not be considered, by impartial men, as a mere exercise of authority. It is true, the authority of the sovereign would accompany it, and the proceeding would be so conducted as that the honour of his government should be preserved; but the grand character of the message would be mercy. Neither would the goodness of it be diminished by the authority which attended it, nor by the malignant disposition of the parties. Should some of them even prove incorrigible, and be executed as hardened traitors, the mercy of the sovereign in sending the message, would be just the same. *They* might possibly object, that the government which they had resisted was hard and rigid; that their parents before them had always disliked it, and had taught them from their childhood to despise it; that to require them to embrace *with all their hearts* a message, the very import of which was, that they had transgressed *without cause, and deserved to die*, was too humiliating for flesh and blood to bear; and that, if he would not pardon them without their cordially subscribing to such an instrument, he had better have left them to die as they were; for, instead of its being good news to them, it would prove the means of aggravating their misery. Every loyal subject, however, would easily perceive that it *was* good news, and a great instance of mercy, however they might treat it, and of whatever evil, through their perverseness, it might be the occasion.

If faith in Christ be the duty of the ungodly, it must, of course, follow, that every sinner, whatever be his character, is completely *warranted* to trust in the Lord Jesus Christ for the salvation of his soul. In other words, he has every possible encouragement to relinquish his former attachment and confidences, and to commit his soul into the hands of Jesus to be saved. If believing in Christ be a privilege belonging only to the regenerate, and no sinner, while unregenerate, be warranted to exercise it, it will follow, either that a sinner may know himself to be regenerate before he believes, or that the first exercise of faith is an act of presumption. That the bias of the heart requires to be turned to God antecedently to believing, has been admitted; because the nature of believing is such, that it cannot be exercised while the soul is under the dominion of wilful blindness, hardness, and aversion. These dispositions are represented in the Scriptures as a bar in the way of faith, as being inconsistent with it;[1] and which, consequently, need to be taken out of the way. But, whatever necessity there may be for a change of heart in order to believing, it is neither necessary nor possible that the party should be *conscious* of it until he has believed. It is necessary that the eyes of a blind man should be opened, before he can see; but it is neither necessary nor possible for him to know that his eyes are open until he does see. It is only by surrounding objects appearing to his view, that he knows the obstructing film to be removed. But, if regeneration be necessary to *warrant* believing, and yet it be impossible to obtain a consciousness of it until we have believed, it follows that the first exercise of faith is without foundation; that is, it is not faith, but presumption.

If believing be the *duty* of every sinner to whom the Gospel is preached, there can be no doubt as to a *warrant* for it, whatever be his character; and to maintain the latter, without admitting the former, would be reducing it to a mere matter of discretion. It might be *inexpedient* to reject the way of salvation, but it could not be *unlawful*.

Second: Though believing in Christ is a compliance with a duty, yet it is not *as a duty*, or by way of *reward* for a virtuous act, that we

---

1. See Proposition IV on page 38.

are said to be *justified by it.* It is true, God does reward the services of his people, as the Scriptures abundantly teach; but this *follows* upon justification. We must stand accepted in the beloved, before our services can be acceptable or rewardable. Moreover, if we were justified by faith as a *duty,* justification *by faith* could not be, as it is, opposed to justification *by works: To him that worketh is the reward not reckoned of grace, but of debt. But to him that worketh not, but believeth on him that justifeth the ungodly, his faith is counted for right-eousness,* (Romans 4:2-5). The Scripture doctrine of *justification by faith,* in opposition to the works of the law, appears to me as follows: − By believing in Jesus Christ, the sinner becomes vitally *united* to him, or, as the Scriptures express it, *joined to the Lord,* and is of *one spirit with him,* (1 Corinthians 6:17): and this union, according to the divine constitution, as revealed in the Gospel, is the ground of an interest in his righteousness. Agreeable to this is the following language: − *There is therefore now* NO CONDEMNATION *to them which are* IN *Christ Jesus. − Of him are ye in Christ Jesus, who of God is made unto us wisdom and* RIGHTEOUSNESS, *etc. − That I may be found* IN *him, not having mine own righteousness, which is of the law, but that which is through the faith of Christ.* (Romans 8:1; 1 Corinthians 1:30; Philippians 3:9). As the union which, in the order of nature, precedes a revealed interest in Christ's righteousness, is spoken of in allusion to that of marriage, the one may serve to illustrate the other. A rich and generous character, walking in the fields, espies a forlorn female infant, deserted by some unfeeling parent in the day that it was born, and left to perish. He sees its helpless condition, and resolves to save it. Under his kind patronage, the child grows up to maturity. He now resolves to make her his wife, and marries her in legal form, and she becomes his wife. She is now, according to the public statutes of the realm, interested in all his possessions. Great is the transition! Ask her, in the height of her glory, how she became possessed of all this wealth; and, if she retains a proper spirit, she will answer in some such manner as this: "It was not mine, but my deliverer's − his who rescued me from death. It is no reward of any good deeds on my part. It is *by marriage.* It is *of grace.*"

It is easy to perceive, in this case, that it was necessary that she should be voluntarily married to her husband, before she could, according to the public statutes of the realm, be interested in his possessions, and that she now enjoys those possessions *by marriage;* yet who would think of asserting that her consenting to be his wife was a meritorious act, and that all his possessions were given her as the reward of it?

Third: From the foregoing view of things, we may perceive *the alarming situation of unbelievers.* By unbelievers, I mean not only avowed infidels, but all persons who hear, or have opportunity to hear, the Gospel, or to come at the knowledge of what is taught in the Holy Scriptures, and do not cordially embrace it. It is an alarming thought to be a *sinner* against the greatest and best of Beings; but to be an *unbelieving sinner* is much more so. There is deliverance from *the curse of the law,* through Him who was *made a curse for us.* But if, like the barren fig-tree, we stand, from year to year, under Gospel culture, and bear no fruit, we may expect to fall under the curse of the Saviour; and who is to deliver us from this? *If the word spoken by angels was steadfast, and every transgression and disobedience received a just recompence of reward; how shall we escape, if we neglect so* GREAT *salvation?* (*Hebrew 2:2, 3*).

We are in the habit of pitying heathens, who are enthralled by abominable superstition, and immersed in the immoralities which accompany it; but to live in the midst of Gospel light, and reject it, or even disregard it, is abundantly more criminal, and will be followed with a heavier punishment. We feel for the condition of profligate characters – for swearers, and drunkards, and fornicators, and liars, and thieves, and murderers; but these crimes become tenfold more heinous, in being committed under the light of revelation, and in contempt of all the warnings and gracious invitations of the Gospel. The most profligate character, who never possessed these advantages, may be far less criminal in the sight of God than the most sober and decent, who possesses, and disregards them. It was on this principle that such a heavy woe was denounced against Chorazin and Bethsaida, and that their sin was represented as exceeding that of Sodom.

The Gospel wears an aspect of mercy towards sinners; but towards unbelieving sinners, the Scriptures deal wholly in the language of threatening. *I am come,* saith our Saviour, *a light into the world, that whosoever believeth on me should not abide in darkness.* AND IF ANY

MAN HEAR MY WORDS, AND BELIEVE NOT, *I judge him not,* [that is, not at present;] *for I came not to judge the world, but to save the world. He that rejecteth me, and receiveth not my words, hath one that judgeth him: the word that I have spoken, the same shall judge him in the last day. (John 12:46-48).* It will be of but small account, in that day, that we have escaped a few of the *lusts of the flesh,* if we have been led captive by those of the *mind.* If the greatest gift of Heaven be set at nought by us, through the pride of science, or a vain conceit of our own righteousness, how shall we stand when He appeareth?

It will then be found that a price was in our hands to get wisdom, but that we had no *heart to it;* and that herein consists our sin, and from hence proceeds our ruin. God called, and we would not hearken; he stretched out his hand, and no man regarded: therefore he will laugh at our calamity, and mock when our fear cometh. It is intimated, both in the Old and New Testaments, that the recollection of the means of salvation having been within our reach, will be a bitter aggravation to our punishment. *They come unto thee,* saith the Lord to Ezekiel, *as the people cometh, and they sit before thee as my people, and they hear thy words, but they will not do them ... And when this cometh to pass, (lo, it will come!)* THEN SHALL THEY KNOW THAT A PROPHET HATH BEEN AMONG THEM. (*Ezekiel 33:31-33*). To the same purpose, our Saviour speaks of those who should reject the doctrine of his apostles. *Into whatsoever city ye enter, and they receive you not, go your ways out into the streets of the same, and say, Even the very dust of your city, which cleaveth on us, we do wipe off against you:* NOTWITHSTANDING BE YE SURE OF THIS, THAT THE KINGDOM OF GOD IS COME NIGH UNTO YOU. (*Luke 10:10, 11*).

Great as is the sin of unbelief, however, it is not unpardonable. It becomes such only by persisting in it until death. Saul of Tarsus was an unbeliever; yet he *obtained mercy.* And his being an unbeliever, rather than a presumptuous opposer of Christ against conviction, placed him within the pale of forgiveness, and is, therefore, assigned as a reason of it. (*1 Timothy 1:13*).

This consideration affords a hope even to unbelievers. O ye self-righteous despisers of a free salvation through a Mediator, be it known to you that there is no other name given under heaven, or among men, by which you can be saved. To him whom you have disregarded and despised, you must, either voluntarily or involuntarily, submit: *To him every knee shall bow.* You cannot go back into a state of non-existence, however desirable it might be to many of you; for God hath stamped immortality upon your natures. You cannot turn to the right hand, nor to the left, with any advantage. Whether you give a loose to your inclination, or put a force upon it by an assumed devotion, each will lead to the same issue. Neither can you stand still. Like a vessel in a tempestuous ocean, you must go this way or that; and, go which way you will, if it be not to Jesus, as utterly unworthy, you are only heaping up wrath against the day of wrath. Whether you sing, or pray, or hear, or preach, or feed the poor, or till the soil, if *self* be your object, and *Christ* be disregarded, all is sin, (*Proverbs 15:8, 9; 28:9; 21:4*), and will all issue in disappointment: *The root is rottenness, and the blossom shall go up as the dust.* Whither will you go? Jesus invites you to come to him. His servants beseech you, in his name, to be reconciled to God. The Spirit saith, *Come;* and the bride saith, *Come;* and *whosoever will, let him come, and take of the water of life freely.* An eternal heaven is before you, in one direction, and an eternal hell in the other. Your answer is required. Be one thing or another. Choose you this day whom ye will serve. For our part, we will abide by our Lord and Saviour. If you continue to reject him, so it must be. *Nevertheless, be ye sure of this, that the kingdom of God has come* NIGH *unto you.*

Finally: *From what has been advanced, we may form a judgement of our duty, as ministers of the word, in dealing with the unconverted.* The work of the Christian ministry, it has been said, is to *preach the Gospel,* or to hold up the free grace of God through Jesus Christ, as the only way of a sinner's salvation. This is, doubtless, true; and if this be not the leading theme of our ministrations, we had better be anything than preachers. *Woe unto us, if we preach not the Gospel!* The minister who, under a pretence of pressing the practice of religion, neglects its all-important principles, labours in the fire. He may enforce duty till duty freezes upon his lips. Neither his hearers nor himself will greatly regard it. But, on the contrary, if, by *preaching the Gospel,* be meant the insisting solely upon the blessings and privileges of religion, to the neglect of exhortations, calls, and warnings, it is sufficient to say that such was not the practice of Christ and his apostles. It will not be denied that they preached the Gospel; yet they warned, admonished, and entreated sinners to *repent and believe; to believe while they had the light; to labour not for the meat that perisheth, but for that meat which endureth unto everlasting life; to repent, and be converted, that their sins might be blotted out; to come to the marriage supper, for that all things were ready;* in summary, *to be reconciled unto God.*

If the inability of sinners to perform things spiritually good were natural, or such as existed independent of their present choice, it would be absurd and cruel to address them in such language. No one in his right mind would think of calling the blind to look, the deaf to hear, or the dead to rise up and walk, and of threatening them with punishment in case of their refusal. But, if the blindness arise from the love of darkness rather than light; if the deafness resemble that of the adder, which stoppeth her ear, and will not hear the voice of the charmer, charm he never so wisely; and if the death consist in alienation of heart from God, and the absence of all desire after him; there is no absurdity or cruelty in such addresses.

But enforcing the duties of religion, either on sinners or saints, is, by some, called *preaching the law.* If it were so, it is enough for us that such was the preaching of Christ and his apostles. It is folly and presumption to affect to be more evangelical than they were. All practical preaching, however, is not preaching the law. That alone, I apprehend, ought to be censured as preaching the law in which our acceptance with God is, in some way or other, placed to the account of our obedience to its precepts. When eternal life is represented as the reward of repentance, faith, and sincere obedience, (as it too frequently is, and that under the accommodating form of being '*through* the merits of Christ,') this is preaching the law, and not the Gospel. But the precepts of the law may be illustrated and enforced for evangelical purposes; as tending to vindicate the divine character and government; to convince of sin; to show the necessity of a Saviour, with the freeness of salvation; to ascertain the nature of true religion; and to point out the rule of Christian conduct. Such a way of introducing the divine law, in subservience to the Gospel, is, properly speaking, preaching the Gospel; for the end denominates the action.

If the foregoing principles be just, it is the duty of ministers not only to exhort their unsaved hearers to believe in Jesus Christ for the salvation of their souls; BUT IT IS AT OUR PERIL TO EXHORT THEM TO ANYTHING SHORT OF IT, OR WHICH DOES NOT INVOLVE OR IMPLY IT. I am aware that such an idea may startle many of my readers, and some who are engaged in the Christian ministry. We have sunk into such a compromising way of dealing with the unconverted, as to have well-nigh lost the spirit of the primitive preachers; and hence it is that sinners of every description can sit so quietly as they do, year after year, in our places of worship. It was not so with the hearers of Peter and Paul. They were either *pricked in the heart* in one way, or *cut to the heart* in another. Their preaching commended itself to *every man's conscience in the sight of God.* How shall we account for this difference? Is there not some important error or defect in our ministrations? I have no reference to the preaching of those who disown the divinity or atonement of Christ, on the one hand, whose sermons are little more than harangues on morality; nor to that of gross Antinomians, on the other, whose chief business it is to feed the vanity and malignity of one part of their audience, and the sin-extenuating principles of the other. These are errors, the folly of which is *manifest to all men* who pay any serious regard to the religion of the New Testament. I refer to those who are commonly reputed *evangelical,* and who approve of addresses to the unconverted. I hope no apology is necessary for an attempt to exhibit the Scriptural manner of preaching. If it affects the labours of some of my brethren, I cannot deny but that it may also affect my own. I conceive there is scarcely a minister amongst us, whose preaching has not been more or less influenced by the lethargic systems of the age.

Christ and his apostles, without any hesitation, called on sinners to *repent, and believe the Gospel;* but we, considering them as poor, impotent, and depraved creatures, have been disposed to drop this part of the Christian ministry. Some may have felt afraid of being accounted legal; others have really thought it inconsistent. Considering such things as beyond the *power* of their hearers, they seem to have contented themselves with pressing on them things which they *could* perform, while still continuing the enemies of Christ – such as behaving decently in society, reading the Scriptures, and attending the means of grace. Thus it is that hearers of this description sit at ease in our congregations. Having done their duty, the minister has nothing more to say to them – nothing, however, unless it be to tell them occasionally that something more is *neces-sary* to salvation. But as this implies no guilt on their part, they sit unconcerned, conceiving that all that is required of them is, "to lie in the way, and to wait the Lord's time." But is this the religion of the Scriptures? Where does it appear that the prophets or apostles ever treated that kind of inability which is merely the effect of reigning aversion, as affording any excuse? And where have they descended in their exhortations to things which might be done, and the parties still continue the enemies of God? Instead of leaving out everything of a spiritual nature, because their hearers *could* not find in their hearts to comply with it, it may safely be affirmed, they exhorted to *nothing else*, – treating such inability not only as of *no account*, with regard to the lessening of obligation, but as rendering the subjects of it worthy of the severest rebuke. *To whom shall I speak, and give warning, that they may hear? Behold, their ear is uncircumcised, and they* CANNOT *hearken: behold, the word of the Lord is unto them a reproach; they have no delight in it.* What then? Did the prophet desist from his work, and exhort them to something to which, in their present state of mind, they *could* hearken? Far from it. He delivers his message, whether they would hear, or whether they would forbear: *Thus saith the Lord, Stand ye in the ways, and see, and ask for the old paths, where is the good way, and walk therein, and ye shall find rest for your souls. But they said, We will not walk therein.* And did this induce him to desist? No. He proceeds to read their doom, and calls the world to witness its jus-tice: *Hear, O earth: behold, I will bring evil upon this people, even the fruit of their thoughts, because they have not hearkened unto my words, nor to my law, but rejected it, (Jeremiah 6:10-19).* Many of those who attended the ministry of Christ, were of the same spirit. Their *eyes were blinded*, and their hearts hardened, so that they COULD NOT BELIEVE; yet, paying no manner of regard to this kind of inability, he exhorted them *to believe in the light while they had the light.* And when they had heard, and believed not, he proceeded, without hes-itation, to declare, *He that rejecteth me, and receiveth not my words, hath one that judgeth him: the word that I have spoken, the same shall judge him in the last day, (John 12:36-48).*

Such, also, were many of Paul's hearers at Rome. They *believed not.* But did Paul, seeing they could not receive the Gospel, recommend to them something which they *could* receive? No. He gave them one word at parting: *Well spake the Holy Ghost by Esaias the prophet unto our fathers, saying, Go unto this people, and say, Hearing ye shall hear, and shall not understand; and seeing ye shall see, and not perceive: for the heart of this people is waxed gross, and their ears are dull of hearing, and their eyes have they closed; lest they should see with their eyes, and hear with their ears, and understand with their heart, and should be converted, and I should heal them. Be it known therefore unto you, that the salvation of God is sent unto the Gentiles, and that they will hear it.* (*Acts 28:24-28*).

When did Jesus, or his apostles, go about merely to form the *manners* of men? Where do they exhort to duties which a man may comply with, and yet miss of the kingdom of heaven? If a man *kept their sayings*, he was assured that he should *never see death*. In addressing the unconverted, they began by admonishing them to repent, and believe the Gospel; and, in the course of their labours, exhorted to all manner of duties. But all were to be done *spiritually*, or they would not have acknowledged them to have been done at all. Carnal duties, or duties to be performed otherwise than *to the glory of God*, had no place in their system.

The answer of our Lord to those carnal Jews who inquired of him *what they must do to work the works of God*, is worthy of special notice. Did Jesus give them to understand, that, as to believing in him, however willing they might be, it was a matter entirely beyond their power? that all the directions he had to give were, that they should attend the means, and wait for the moving of the waters? No. Jesus answered, *This is the work of God, that ye believe on him whom he hath sent.* (*John 6:29*). This was the *gate at the head of the way*, as the author of *The Pilgrim's Progress* has admirably represented it, to which sinners must be directed. A *worldly-wise* instructor may inculcate other duties; but the true *evangelist*, after the example of his Lord, will point to this as the first concern, and as that upon which everything else depends.

There is another species of preaching, which proceeds upon much the same principle. Repentance towards God, and faith towards our Lord Jesus Christ, are allowed to be duties, but not *immediate* duties. The sinner is considered as *unable* to comply with them, and therefore they are not urged upon him; but, instead of them, he is directed to *pray for the Holy Spirit, to enable him to repent and believe;* and this, it seems, he *can* do, notwithstanding the aversion of his heart from everything of the kind. But, if any man be required to pray for the Holy Spirit, it must be either sincerely, and in the name of Jesus, or insincerely, and in some other way. The latter, I suppose, will be allowed to be an abomination in the sight of God. He cannot, therefore, be required to do this; and, as to the former, it is just as difficult, and as opposite to the carnal heart, as repentance and faith themselves. Indeed, it amounts to the same thing; for a sincere desire after a spiritual blessing, presented in the name of Jesus, is no other than *the prayer of faith.*

Peter exhorted Simon to pray, not with an impenitent heart, that he might obtain repentance, but with a penitent one, that he might obtain *forgiveness;* and this, no doubt, in the only way in which it was to be obtained, *through Jesus Christ.* REPENT, says he, *and pray to God, if perhaps the thought of thine heart may be forgiven thee.* Our Saviour directed his disciples to pray for the Holy Spirit; but surely the prayer which they were encouraged to offer was to be *sincere,* and with an eye to the Saviour; that is, it was *the prayer of faith,* and therefore could not be a duty directed to be performed antecedently, and in order to the obtaining of it.

The mischief arising from this way of preaching is considerable. *First:* It gives up a very important question to the sinner, even that question which is at issue between God and conscience, on the one hand, and a self-righteous heart, on the other, – namely, whether he be obliged *immediately* to repent, and believe the Gospel. "I could find nothing in the Scriptures," says he, "that would give me any comfort in my present condition – nothing short of *repent, and believe,* which are things I *cannot* comply with; but I have gained it from my good minister. Now my heart is at ease. I am not obliged *immediately* to repent, and sue for mercy in the name of Jesus. It is not, therefore, my sin that I do not. All I am obliged to is, to pray to God to help me to do so; and that I do." Thus, after a bitter conflict with Scripture and conscience, which have pursued him through all his windings, and pressed upon him the call of the Gospel, he finds a shelter in the house of God! Such counsel, instead of aiding the sinner's convictions, (which, as *labourers with God,* is our proper business,) has many a time been equal to a victory over them, or, at least, to the purchase of an armistice. *Second:* It *deceives* the soul. He understands it as a compromise, and so acts upon it. For, though he be, in fact, as far from sincerely praying for repentance, as from repenting, and just as unable to desire faith in Christ, as to exercise it, yet he does not think so. He reckons himself *very* desirous of these things. The reason is, he takes that indirect desire after them, which consists in wishing to be converted, (or anything, however disagreeable in itself,) that he may escape the wrath to come, to be the desire of grace; and, being conscious of possessing this, he considers himself in a fair way, at least, of being converted. Thus he deceives his soul; and thus he is helped forward in his delusion! Nor is this all. He feels himself set at liberty from the *hard* requirement of *returning immediately to God, by Jesus Christ, as utterly unworthy;* and being told to pray that he may be enabled to do so, he supposes that such prayer will avail him, or that God will give him the power of repenting and believing, in answer to his prayers – prayers, be it observed, which must necessarily be offered up with an impenitent, unbelieving heart. This just suits his self-righteous spirit; but, alas! all is delusion.

"You have no relief, then," say some, "for the sinner?" I answer, If the Gospel, or any of its blessings, will relieve him, there is no want of relief. But, if there be nothing in Christ, or grace, or heaven, that will suit his inclination, it is not for me to furnish him with anything else, or to encourage him to hope that things will come to a good issue. The only possible way of relieving a sinner, while his heart is averse from God, is by lowering the requirements of Heaven to meet his inclination, or in some way to model the Gospel to his mind. But to relieve him in this manner, is at my peril! If I were commissioned to address a company of men who had engaged in an unprovoked rebellion against their king and country, what ought I to say to them? I might make use of authority or entreaty, as occasion might require; I might caution, warn, threaten, or persuade them; but there would be a point from which I must not depart: *Be ye reconciled to your rightful sovereign;* lay down your arms, and submit to mercy! To this I must inviolably adhere. They might allege that they could not comply with such hard terms. Should I admit their plea, and direct them only to such conduct as might consist with a rebellious spirit, instead of recovering them from rebellion, I should go far towards denominating myself a rebel.

And, as Christ and his apostles never appear to have exhorted the unconverted to anything which did not include or imply repentance and faith, so, *in all their explications of the divine law, and preaching against particular sins, their object was to bring the sinner to this issue.* Though they directed them to no means, in order to get a penitent and believing heart, but to repentance and faith themselves, yet they *used means with them* for that purpose. Thus, our Lord expounded the law in his Sermon on the Mount, and concluded by enforcing such a *hearing of his sayings, and doing them*, as should be equal to *digging deep, and building one's house upon a rock*. And thus the apostle Peter, having charged his countrymen with the murder of the Lord of glory, presently brings it to this issue: *Repent ye therefore, and be converted, that your sins may be blotted out. (Matthew 5–7; Acts 3:14-19).*

Some years ago, I met with a passage in Dr Owen on this subject, which, at that time, sank deep into my heart; and the more observation I have since made, the more just his remarks appear. "It is the duty of ministers," says he, "to plead with men about their sins, but always remember that it be done with that which is the proper end of law and Gospel; that is, that they make use of the sin they speak against to the discovery of the *state* and *condition* wherein the sinner is. Otherwise, haply, they may work men to formality, and hypocrisy, and but little of the true end of preaching the Gospel will be brought about. It will not avail to beat a man off from his drunkenness into a sober formality. A skilful master of the assemblies lays his axe at the root – drives still at the heart. To inveigh against particular sins of ignorant, unregenerate persons, such as the land is full of, is a good work; but yet, though it may be done with great efficacy, vigour, and success, if this be all the effect of it, that they are set upon the most sedulous endeavours of mortifying their sins preached down, all that is done is but like the beating of an enemy in an open field, and driving him into an impregnable castle, not to be prevailed against. Get you, at any time, a sinner at the advantage on the account of any one sin whatever; have you anything to take hold of him by, bring it to his *state* and *condition*; drive it up to the head, and there deal with him. To break men off from particular sins, and not to break their hearts, is to deprive ourselves of advantages of dealing with them." [2]

---

2. *On the Mortification of Sin*, chapter 7.

When a sinner is first seized with conviction, it is natural to suppose that he will abstain from many of his outward vices, though it be only for the quiet of his own mind. But it is not for us to administer comfort to him on this ground, as though, because he had *broken off* a few of *his sins*, he must needs have broken them off *by righteousness*, and either be in the road to life, or, at least, in a fair way of getting into it. It is one of the devices of Satan to alarm the sinner, and fill him with anxiety for the healing of outward eruptions of sin, while the inward part is overlooked, though it be nothing but sin. But we must not be aiding and abetting in these deceptions, nor administer any other relief than that which is held out in the Gospel to sinners, *as sinners*. And when we see such characters violating their promises, and falling anew into their old sins, (which is frequently the case,) instead of joining with them in lamenting the event, and assisting them in healing the wound by renewed efforts of watchfulness, it becomes us, rather, to probe the wound, to make *use* of that which has appeared, for the detecting of that which has not appeared, and so to point them to the blood that cleanses from all sin. "Poor soul!" says the eminent writer just quoted, "it is not thy sore finger, but thy hectic fever, from whence thy life is in danger!" If the cause be removed, the effects will cease. If the spring be purified, the waters will be healed, and the barren ground become productive.

I conclude with a few remarks on the *order* of addressing exhortations to the unconverted. There being an established order in the workings of the human mind, it has been made a question, whether the same ought not to be preserved in addressing it. As for instance: we cannot be convinced of sin, without previous ideas of God and moral government; nor of the need of a Saviour, without being convinced of sin; nor of the importance of salvation, without suitable conceptions of sin's evil nature. Hence, it may be supposed we ought not to teach any one of these truths until the preceding one is well understood; or, at least, that we ought not to preach the Gospel without prefacing it by representing the just requirements of the law, our state as sinners, and the impossibility of being justified by the works of our hands. Doubtless such representations are proper and necessary; but not so necessary as to render it improper, on any occasion, to introduce the doctrine of the Gospel without them, and much less to refrain from teaching it until they are understood and felt. In this case, a minister must be reduced to the greatest perplexity, never knowing when it was safe to introduce the salvation of Christ, lest some of his hearers should not be sufficiently prepared to receive it. The truth is, it is *never* unsafe to introduce this doctrine. There is such a connection in divine truth, that, if any one part of it reaches the mind, and finds a place in the heart, all others which may precede it in the order of things, will come in along with it. In receiving a doctrine, we receive not only what is expressed, but what is *implied* by it; and thus the doctrine of the cross may *itself* be the means of convincing us of the evil of sin. An example of this lately occurred in the experience of a child of eleven years of age. Her minister, visiting her under a threatening affliction, and perceiving her to be unaffected with her sinful condition, suggested that "it was no small matter that brought down the Lord of glory into this world, to suffer and die; there must be something very offensive in the nature of sin against a holy God." This remark appears to have sunk into her heart, and to have issued in a saving change. [3] Divine truths are like chain-shot: they go together, and we need not perplex ourselves which should enter first. If any one enter, it will draw the rest after it.

Remarks nearly similar may be made concerning *duties*. Though the Scriptures know nothing of duties to be performed without faith, or which do not *include* or *imply* it, yet they do not wait for the sinner's being possessed of faith, before they exhort him to other spiritual exercises, such as *seeking* the Lord, *loving* him, *serving* him, etc; nor need we lay any such restraints upon ourselves. Such is the *connection* of the duties as well as the truths of religion, that, if one be truly complied with, we need not fear that the others will be wanting. If God be sought, loved, or served, we may be sure that Jesus is embraced; and, if Jesus be embraced, that sin is abhorred. Or, should things first occur to the mind in another order – should sin be the immediate object of our thoughts, – if this be abhorred, the God against whom it is committed must, at the same instant, be loved; and the Saviour, who was made a sacrifice to deliver us from it, embraced. Let any part of truth or holiness but find a place in the heart, and the rest will be with it. Those parts which, in the order of things, are required to precede it, will come in by way of *implication;* and those which follow it, will be *produced* by it. Thus the primitive preachers

---

3. *Dying Exercises of Susannah Wright, of Weekly, near Kettering.*

seem to have had none of that scrupulosity which appears in the discourses and writings of some modern preachers. Sometimes, they exhorted sinners to *believe* in Jesus; but it was such belief as *implied* repentance for sin; sometimes, to *repent, and be converted;* but it was such repentance and conversion as included believing; and, sometimes, to *labour for the meat that endureth unto everlasting life;* but it was such labouring as comprehended both repentance and faith.

Some have inferred from the doctrine of justification by faith, in opposition to the works of the law, that sinners ought not to be exhorted to anything which comprises obedience to the law, either in heart or life, except we should preach the law to them for the purpose of conviction; and this, lest we should be found directing them to the works of their own hands, as the ground of acceptance with God. From the same principle, it has been concluded, that faith itself cannot include any holy disposition of the heart, because all holy dispositions contain obedience to the law. If this reasoning be just, all exhorting of sinners to things expressive of a holy exercise of heart, is either improper, or requires to be understood as merely preaching the law for the purpose of conviction; as our Saviour directed the young ruler to *keep the commandments if he would enter into life.* Yet the Scriptures abound with such exhortations. Sinners are exhorted to *seek* God, to *serve* him with fear and joy, to *forsake* their wicked way, and *return* to him, to *repent,* and *be converted.* These are manifestly exercises of the heart, and addressed to the unconverted. Neither are they to be understood as the requirements of a covenant of works. That covenant neither requires repentance, nor promises forgiveness. But sinners are directed to these things under a promise of *mercy* and *abundant pardon.* There is a wide difference between these addresses and the address of our Lord to the young ruler: that to which he was directed was the producing of a righteousness adequate to the demands of the law, which was naturally impossible; and our Lord's design was to show its impossibility, and thereby to convince him of the need of Gospel mercy: but that to which the above directions point, is not to any natural impossibility, but to the very way of mercy. The manner in which the primitive preachers guarded against self-righteousness was very different from this. They were not afraid of exhorting either saints or sinners to holy exercises of heart, nor of connecting with them the promises of mercy. But, though they exhibited the promises of eternal life to any and every spiritual exercise, yet they never taught that it was on account of it; but of mere grace, through the redemption that is in Jesus Christ. The ground on which they took their stand was, *Cursed is every one that continueth not in all things which are written in the book of the law to do them.* (*Galatians 3:10*). From hence they inferred the impossibility of a sinner being justified, in any other way than for the sake of him who was *made a curse for us;* and, from hence, it clearly follows, that, whatever holiness any sinner may possess, before, in, or after believing, it is of no account whatever, as a ground of acceptance with God. If we inculcate *this* doctrine, we need not fear exhorting sinners to holy exercises of heart, nor holding up the promises of mercy to all who thus return to God by Jesus Christ.

– THE END –

Made in the USA
Coppell, TX
29 December 2025

67678465R00063